Competition and Growth

Zeuthen Lecture Book Series
Karl Gunnar Persson, editor

Competition and Growth

Reconciling Theory and Evidence

Philippe Aghion and
Rachel Griffith

The MIT Press
Cambridge, Massachusetts
London, England

MIT Press books may be purchased at special quantity discounts for business or sales promotional use. For information, please email special_sales@mitpress.mit.edu or write to Special Sales Department, The MIT Press, 5 Cambridge Center, Cambridge, MA 02142.

This book was set in Palatino on 3B2 by Asco Typesetters, Hong Kong, and was printed and bound in the United States of America.

Library of Congress Cataloging-in-Publication Data

Aghion, Philippe
  Competition and growth : reconciling theory and evidence / Philippe Aghion and Rachel Griffith.
    p.   cm. — (Zeuthen lecture book series)
  Includes bibliographical references and index.
  ISBN 0-262-01218-9 (alk. paper)
  1. Competition—Government policy. 2. Economic development. I. Griffith, Rachel. II. Title. III. Series.
  HD41.A37   2005
  338.9′001—dc22   2005042801

10 9 8 7 6 5 4 3 2 1

Contents

Series Foreword

The Zeuthen Lectures offer a forum for leading scholars to develop and synthesize novel results in theoretical and applied economics. They aim to present advances in knowledge in a form accessible to a wide audience of economists and advanced students of economics. The choice of topics will range from abstract theorizing to economic history. Regardless of the topic, the emphasis in the lecture series will be on originality and relevance. The Zeuthen Lectures are organized by the Institute of Economics, University of Copenhagen.

The lecture series is named after Frederik Zeuthen, a former professor at the Institute of Economics.

Karl Gunnar Persson

Acknowledgments

This book owes its existence to Birgit Grodal and Gunnar Persson of the University of Copenhagen, who invited us to give the Zeuthen Lectures in November 2001. It is only natural that it be dedicated to the memory of Birgit Grodal, who stands to us and to many economists of all generations as a model of scientific achievement and integrity, and as an institution-builder who devoted all her intelligence and generosity to promote top-level economics in Europe.

This book is also the story of an applied theorist (Philippe Aghion) and an applied econometrician (Rachel Griffith) who first performed parallel work on competition and innovation leading to partly contradictory results, then decided to confront their results and to look for extended paradigms and new estimation techniques that would overcome the initial discrepancies between theory and empirics and at the same time provide a new approach to thinking about policy issues.

The book would never have been without our collaborations with exceptional co-authors. We are particularly indebted to Peter Howitt and Richard Blundell, who contributed to the book in a fundamental way, respectively to the theory and the empirics developed in all the chapters. We have learned and continue to learn so much from them, and they stand to us as permanent sources of inspiration and wisdom. We are also very grateful to our other co-authors on the various work covered in the book, namely John Van Reenen and Mark Schankerman on chapter 1, Mathias Dewatripont and Patrick Rey on chapter 2, Nick Bloom, Christopher Harris, and John Vickers on chapter 3, and Robin Burgess, Susanne Prantl, Stephen Redding, and Fabrizio Zilibotti on chapter 4.

Finally, our thinking on competition and growth, greatly benefited from intense discussions over the past fourteen years and also from joint work with Daron Acemoglu, Beatriz Armendáriz, Patrick Bolton,

Jan Boone, Wendy Carlin, Richard Caves, David Encaoua, Rupert Harrison, Oliver Hart, Elhanan Helpman, Stephen Nickell, Ariel Pakes, Helen Simpson, Robert Solow, Jean Tirole, David Ulph, and Xavier Vives, and from the invaluable feedback we got from our students when we taught the material of these lectures both at Harvard and at University College London. We would particularly like to thank Rupert Harrison for reading through a complete draft of this book and making many substantive and stylistic suggestions.

Introduction

The view that competition and entry should promote efficiency and prosperity has now become a common wisdom worldwide. However, looking back only forty years, one finds a very different consensus among economic observers and policymakers. Latin American countries were pursuing import substitution policies, which allowed countries like Peru, Brazil, or Mexico to double their per capita GDP levels relative to the United States between 1945 and the early 1970s.[1] Southeast Asian countries and Japan were emphasizing export promotion and proactive industrial policies, which allowed them to grow at an annual growth rate of above 6 percent on average until the mid-1990s. Finally, European countries had granted legal monopolies to large domestic firms yet were rapidly catching up with U.S. productivity levels up until the early 1980s.

But these positive growth trends did not last. Latin American countries experienced chronic instability and stagnation from the 1970s onward. Growth in European Union (EU) countries petered out from the 1980s, with per capita GDP stuck at 70 percent of the U.S. level,[2] and growth performance recently deteriorating, both in absolute terms and in comparison to the United States. Finally, since 1994 the Japanese have faced a deep and prolonged recession that has forced them to reconsider their overall economic model.

Why then, under some circumstances, can high growth be maintained through more protectionist and entrenched policies, whereas under other circumstances growth seems to require higher competition and openness?

A tentative answer to this question, recently put forward by Acemoglu, Aghion, and Zilibotti (2003) and inspired by the work of Gerschenkron (1962), is that there is not one but several engines of growth, which do not require the same institutions or policies. In less developed or middle-income countries, growth relies heavily upon factor accumulation (investment in physical capital, labor, and human capital or education) and upon imitating or adapting technologies from more advanced countries. Both factor accumulation and imitation can prosper under limited competition and entry (this relates to the well-known infant-industry argument). However, in advanced knowledge-based economies, where the growth potential of factor accumulation and imitation have been exhausted, frontier innovation becomes the main source of growth. To the extent that frontier innovation *may* require open markets and free entry, then countries should move from less competitive to more competitive institutions in order to sustain high growth rates throughout the various stages of their development process.

But are we so sure that competition always favors innovation in developed economies? In fact we often hear the opposite view being advocated by prominent innovators—for example, by Microsoft over the past five years—namely, that tough competition discourages innovation and inhibits productivity growth by reducing the expected rents from innovation (economists call this a "rent dissipation" effect of competition). If, as an entrepreneur, I anticipate future antitrust action, or future liberalization of entry in my market, why should I invest so much in new innovations if the rents from these are to be destroyed by new entrants or potential competitors? On the other hand, antitrust practitioners and competition authorities argue that competition is a necessary input into innovation, both because it encourages new entry and because it keeps incumbent firms on their toes and forces them to innovate in order to survive competition. So, who is right and who is wrong? Can one turn to economists for clear and definite views on this debate?

The answer is no. While competition features prominently in the history of economic thought, it is fair to say that economists still have a limited, and sometimes contradictory, understanding of its economic effects and, in particular, of the relationship between competition and growth. What we have accumulated so far are only bits and pieces: on the one hand, theoretical arguments that make predictions of either a positive or negative relationship; on the other hand, contrasting pieces of historical or empirical evidence. From this, a deep feeling of confusion arises. The main purpose of this book is to provide the first serious attempt at putting the various pieces of the puzzle together into a unified and coherent view of where and when one should expect competition policy or the deregulation of entry to boost productivity growth, and when we should expect them to have only limited or even negative effects on growth. What weight should policymakers place on rewarding successful innovation through granting monopoly power versus enhancing the competitive pressures markets place on firms to push forward the frontier? Is there really a trade-off to be made here, or can these policies be used as complementary mechanisms?

This book takes the form of a dialogue between an applied theorist and an econometrician. On the theory side, we build upon "Schumpeterian growth" models in which growth results from entrepreneurial innovations. Innovative activities are induced by the economic environment, and each new innovation destroys the monopoly rents generated by previous innovators. On the empirical side, we illustrate the use of new techniques that have been implemented by applied microeconometricians to analyze the random process of innovation and patenting and to develop adequate measures and instruments for competition and entry. The dialogue between the theory and the econometrics is one in which, at each round or chapter, (1) models are systematically confronted with data, (2) the data either invalidate the models or suggest changes in the modeling strategy, and (3) new predictions emerging from the modified models are again confronted by the data, thereby initiating a new round of interaction between the two sides.

In contrast to previous studies on competition, we deliberately focus on the broad stance that competition policy should take. The voluminous industrial organization (IO) literature details the welfare effects of specific antitrust decisions, each emphasizing a different aspect and pointing to specific effects in different directions. This book focuses on the broader picture. For example, it can help governments in accession countries understand how to both achieve the benefits of tougher competition, while also limiting the negative impact this may have in terms of the dislocation of some sectors or industries. It also produces more coherent policy advice, for example, on the design of patent protection, proactive innovation policy, and competition policy as complementary instruments to foster productivity growth.

We start in chapter 1 by reviewing the early theoretical and empirical literatures. Although highly segmented and often contradictory, these provide foundations for our own approach. In particular, theory pointed to a detrimental effect of competition on innovation and growth, while the empirical literature instead suggested that more competitive market structures are associated with greater innovative output, an idea that had much support in policy circles.

In chapter 2 we explore common wisdom, according to which competition is mainly growth-enhancing because it forces firms to reduce costs and innovate in order to survive. We find that, while this Darwinian view of competition may account for the impact of competition on some aspects of static efficiency, it is not fully vindicated by the data and also does not fully explain the impact of competition on the growth process.

In chapter 3 we explore an alternative route that allows us to both unify the theory and reconcile it more fully with the empirical evidence. We extend the Schumpeterian growth paradigm by distinguishing between *pre-innovation* rents and *post-innovation* rents, and by introducing the notion that innovation is a way to escape competition. More intense competition may lead to more innovation because it reduces pre-innovation rents by more than it reduces post-innovation rents. Whether this "escape competition" effect or the "rent dissipation" effect dominates will turn out to depend upon technological characteristics of a sector or industry. In particular, it will depend on the technological distance between firms in that industry, and which of these two effects dominates in the overall economy will depend upon the distribution of technological characteristics across sectors. Our analysis predicts an inverted-U relationship between competition and innovation, and shows that the prediction is fully consistent with the evidence.

In chapter 4 we introduce entry into the picture and look at the extent to which the effect of liberalizing entry on innovation and productivity growth depends upon the technological distance between the domestic incumbent and the world technology frontier. Reducing barriers to entry to foreign products and firms has an overall positive effect on innovation and productivity growth, but it has a more positive effect on economic performance for firms and industries that are initially closer to the technological frontier. In contrast, performance in firms and industries that are initially far from the frontier may actually be damaged by liberalization. The reason is that incumbent firms that are sufficiently close to the technological frontier can survive and deter entry by innovating. In contrast, firms and sectors that are far below the frontier are in a weaker position to fight external entry. For these firms, an increase in the entry threat reduces the expected payoff from innovating, since their expected life horizon has become shorter. Another finding is that the institutional environment in which firms function, has a central bearing on whether or not they benefit from liberalization. Thus, in relative terms, trade reforms hurt growth in regions with pro-labor regulations, while enhancing growth in regions with pro-employer regulations. These predictions are supported by empirical work in the United Kingdom, in India, and in cross-country analysis. They suggest that, for example, accession countries may want to have policies in place to foster the movement of labor out of industries far below the frontier.

Fully self-contained, this book can be read by anyone with an elementary acquaintance with basic economic principles and high school–level algebra.

1   A Divorce between Theory and Empirics

Looking back to the mid-nineties, a curious economic observer seeking to form a coherent view on what impact competition policy had on growth would find herself discouraged by the lack of consensus on the subject. Existing theories were in sharp juxtaposition to both the common wisdom and empirical evidence. On the one hand, she would find that the leading theoretical models in industrial organization or in growth theory predicted that more intense product market competition discourages innovation and growth as it reduces the rents from innovating (the argument used by the Bill Gateses of this world to oppose antitrust action). On the other hand, the common view, dating back to Adam Smith and put forward more recently by economists including Michael Porter, was that competition enhances growth because it exerts pressure on firms to cut costs, reduce slack, and innovate in order to maintain market position, by introducing new products or new production processes. These beliefs resulted in wide-ranging policy initiatives aimed at facilitating competition by promoting openness, free trade, free entry by foreign investors, and monetary integration across the world.

Now why should a serious observer believe the common wisdom if it is not supported by empirical evidence? If she were truly serious, our observer would look to recent econometric studies on the subject, hoping that they would confirm the theories and prove the common wisdom wrong. However, the "state-of-the-art" microeconometric studies of the 1990s would add to her confusion, by pointing to an unambiguously positive correlation between productivity growth and various measures of the intensity of product market competition. In the face of this evidence, she could only be left feeling discomfort with the theory. Yet would she be right to throw out the theory? Or, like the proverbial baby in the bathwater, should more care be taken?

In this chapter, we provide an account of the divide between applied theorists and empiricists in their approach to competition and its effects on growth. In doing so, we try to uncover missing or embryonic elements on either side that could hint at the possibility of a subsequent reconciliation between the different views.

1.1   The Dominant Theories by the Early 1990s

To gain an understanding of the dominant view on competition, innovation, and entry, our observer would naturally consult Tirole's (1988) reference textbook on the theory of industrial organization, then look at the more recent endogenous growth literature (e.g., Romer 1990; Aghion and Howitt 1992; Grossman and Helpman 1991). In this section, we provide a brief account of what our observer would have learned from her theoretical exploration.

1.1.1   The IO Models of Product Differentiation and Price Competition, and the Schumpeterian Effect of Competition

The two leading models of price competition and product differentiation in theoretical IO, are the Hotelling linear model (and the circular version of that model by Salop (1977)) and the symmetric model of monopolistic competition by Dixit and Stiglitz (1977). This latter model has been the template for Romer's (1990) model of endogenous growth with increasing product variety. Both models are described in detail in chapter 7 of Tirole 1988, and they deliver the same prediction: More intense product market competition reduces the rents of those firms that successfully enter the market, and therefore it discourages firms from entering in the first place. Entry in these models is what captures the notion of innovation.

The Circular Model   Salop's circular model, shown in figure 1.1, is one where the market is represented by a circle of unit length, on which firms locate evenly. Thus, if there are n firms in the market, the "distance" between two neighboring firms is $1/n$. Consumers are uniformly distributed over the circle, and they must incur a transportation cost t per unit of length they travel through. This parameter t captures the extent of product market competition. The higher the t, the more costly it is for a consumer to shift from one firm to another, and therefore the less an individual firm on the circle has to worry about the risk that consumers located in her immediate neighborhood be competed

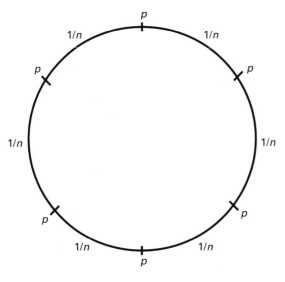

Figure 1.1
Salop circle model

away by other firms, even if the firm sets a price close to its unconstrained monopoly price. Thus, a higher t corresponds to a lower
degree of product market competition.

The timing of the model is as follows. In a first stage, firms with
identical unit production cost c decide whether or not to *enter* the
market, where entry involves a fixed cost f. Think of entry in this
model as capturing the innovation decision of a firm. More entry corresponds to more (product) innovation. In a second stage, those firms
that have entered the market compete in price, that is, engage in Bertrand competition. Our main question is how an increase in product
market competition, modeled as a reduction in t, affects innovation,
measured by entry or the equilibrium number of firms in the market.
The answer turns out to be straightforward and unambiguous, namely,
that increased product market competition discourages entry.

To understand why more formally, we solve the model by backward
induction, first solving for the Nash equilibrium of the price competition game for a given number of firms n in the market, then moving
back to the entry stage and solving for the equilibrium value of n that
makes firms just indifferent between incurring the entry cost f and
staying out of the market. Here we implicitly assume free entry, which
means that firms keep entering the circle until the marginal firm finds

it unprofitable to pay the entry cost f, given the number of firms already on the market.

Price competition: We restrict attention to symmetric Nash equilibria where all firms charge the same price p in equilibrium. If firm i chooses price p_i and all other firms have chosen price p, then the consumers who will be indifferent between purchasing from firm i or its neighbor are located at distance x from firm i on either side, such that

$$p_i + tx = p + t(1/n - x).$$

This implies that the total demand for firm i's product will be

$$D(p_i, p) = 2x = \frac{t/n + p - p_i}{t}.$$

Firm i will thus react to price p by its competitors, by choosing p_i so as to maximize its current profit

$$\pi(p_i, p) = (p_i - c)D(p_i, p).$$

Solving for p_i by taking the first-order condition for this maximization, then using the fact that in a symmetric Nash equilibrium of this price competition game,

$$p_i = p,$$

we obtain the following equilibrium price and profit flows:

$$p^* = \frac{t}{n} + c$$

and

$$\pi^*(n) = \frac{t}{n^2}.$$

Not surprisingly, an increase in product market competition reduces the equilibrium level of profits for firms in the market. In the absence of product differentiation, that is, when $t = 0$, we are back to the traditional Bertrand competition case where profits are competed down to zero.

Entry: Moving back to the initial entry stage, the equilibrium number of firms n^* is determined by the free-entry condition

$$\pi^*(n) = f,$$

which immediately yields

$n^* = \sqrt{t/f}.$

In particular, an increase in product market competition, modeled as a reduction in transportation costs, discourages entry by reducing post-entry rents. As Dasgupta and Stiglitz (1980) have suggested, ex post competition drives out ex ante competition. We refer to this as the Schumpeterian effect of product market competition.

The Dixit-Stiglitz Model A similar conclusion obtains in the Dixit-Stiglitz model of product differentiation, where consumers all share the same utility for the differentiated goods, of the form

$$u(q_1, \ldots, q_n) = \left(\sum_{j=1}^{n} q_j^{\alpha} \right)^{1/\alpha} \tag{1.1}$$

where q_i is quantity of good i consumed. In this model, product market competition is captured by the parameter α, with a higher α corresponding to a higher degree of substitutability between the differentiated products, and therefore to a higher degree of competition between the firms that produce them. We again assume symmetry among differentiated goods producers, with all of them facing the same unit production cost c. Then, we can analyze the same two-stage game as before, where differentiated goods producers first decide whether to pay a fixed entry fee f and enter the market, and then those who entered the market compete in price.

Price competition: We take the total number of firms to be large, so that an individual firm i takes the total amount of consumption

$$\sum_{j=1}^{n} q_j^{\alpha}$$

as given when choosing its price p_i. The inverse demand function for product i is obtained by equating the price p_i of good i to the marginal utility of that good, namely,

$$p_i = \frac{\partial u}{\partial q_i} = q_i^{\alpha-1} \left(\sum_{i=1}^{n} q_i^{\alpha} \right)^{(1/\alpha)-1}, \tag{1.2}$$

so that when we solve for the quantity demanded we get

$D(p_i) = q_i = k p_i^{-1/(1-\alpha)},$

where

$$k = \left(\sum_{j=1}^{n} q_j^{\alpha} \Big/ w \right)^{1/(\alpha-1)}$$

is treated as a constant by each individual firm i for n sufficiently large, and where w denotes the wealth of the representative consumer.

Thus firm i chooses the price p_i that maximizes $(p_i - c_i)p_i^{1/(\alpha-1)}$, which implies

$$p_i = \frac{c}{\alpha},$$

that is, price equals marginal cost scaled up by the degree of substitutability of products. The higher the degree of substitutability, the lower the price. Now, substituting for p_i into equation (2.2), and using the fact that all firms produce the same quantity q in a symmetric Nash equilibrium, we obtain the equilibrium profit

$$\pi^*(n) = (1 - \alpha)\frac{w}{n}.$$

Entry: Once again, the equilibrium level of entry n^* is simply determined by the free-entry condition

$$\pi^*(n) = f.$$

This yields the simple expression

$$n^* = \frac{(1 - \alpha)w}{f},$$

which again shows that an increase in product market competition, here modeled as an increase in the substitutability between the differentiated goods as measured by α, reduces post-entry rents and therefore discourages entry (or innovation). Thus, we again obtain an unambiguously negative Schumpeterian effect of product market competition on innovation.

1.1.2 Two Attempts at Generating a Positive Effect of Competition on Entry or Innovation

Our observer would thus walk away from her exploration of this early IO theory with the idea that more intense competition discourages entry, because it reduces post-entry rents. She would be wrong, however, to think that all IO models of competition and entry or competition and innovation predict a negative impact of competition. In particular, she will have missed two important insights from IO models, namely, the interplay between rent dissipation and preemption incentives, and the differences between vertical (i.e., quality improving) and horizontal innovations. Those insights, which we briefly spell out in this section, will prove to be useful when, in subsequent chapters, we try to reconcile theory with empirical evidence on the relationship between competition and growth.

The Rent Dissipation Effect   Chapters 8 and 10 of Tirole 1988 present closely related models of preemption and innovation,[3] which suggest a positive effect of product market competition on innovation. Suppose, for example, that an incumbent firm is engaged in a race with a potential entrant for a new innovation that will reduce costs. Who will invest more research and development (R&D) resources in the race, the incumbent or the potential entrant? The answer turns out to be ambiguous, and it relies on the trade-off between two opposite effects: a *rent dissipation* effect and a *replacement* effect. The replacement effect, uncovered by Kenneth Arrow in 1962, refers to the fact that, by innovating, the incumbent monopolist replaces her own rents, whereas the potential entrant has no preexisting rents to replace. Everything else remaining equal, this effect will induce the entrant to invest more in the race than the incumbent firm will. On the other hand, the rent dissipation effect refers to the fact that the incumbent may lose more by letting the entrant win the race (she dissipates the difference between her current monopoly rents and the duopoly rents if the entrant innovates) than the potential entrant does by letting the incumbent win the race (he loses the difference between what may be at best duopoly rents if he had won the race and zero if the incumbent wins). The rent dissipation effect may or may not counteract the replacement effect. If it does, then the incumbent ends up investing more in the race than does the potential entrant.

How does this relate to product market competition? To get some preliminary intuition, let us go back to our first model of product differentiation, and consider a firm located at one extreme of a linear city, which faces the risk that a second firm will enter and locate at the other extreme of the city. The linear city is like the circular city analyzed earlier, except that consumers are now uniformly distributed on a segment of length one. We still denote by t the unit transport cost.

The only way the incumbent firm can prevent entry is to use its incumbency advantage and to build a second plant at the other extreme of the line before the entrants does. Suppose that the second firm (the potential entrant) observes what the incumbent does before deciding whether or not to enter, and also whether entry involves a positive sunk cost, f. Then, anticipating (undifferentiated) Bertrand competition with the second plant, and therefore zero profits in case it enters, the second firm will not enter, as entry will lead to a net loss of f.

Of course, the second firm could enter into a race with the incumbent in order to arrive first at the other location. However, there is asymmetry between the two firms' incentives to invest in that race. On the one hand, the incumbent firm will lose

$$\pi^m - \pi^d$$

per unit of time if entry occurs, where π^m denotes the incumbent's monopoly profit flow if she wins the race,[4] and π^d denotes the equilibrium duopoly profit of each firm if the entrant succeeds in locating first at the other extreme of the line. Thus, the incumbent firm's incentive to invest in product innovation at the other end of the segment is proportional to $\pi^m - \pi^d$.

On the other hand, by investing in innovation, the potential entrant raises the chance of moving from zero to π^d, and thus its incentive to invest in innovation is proportional to π^d. Note that the potential entrant, like firms in the previous models of monopolistic competition and entry, moves from zero to something positive, but the positive amount is decreasing with competition. However, unlike in the previous models, the incumbent firm starts with positive profits when deciding whether or not to innovate. This, in turn, makes a big difference, as we will see repeatedly in this book.

The IO literature emphasizes the comparison between $\pi^m - \pi^d$ and π^d, and the fact that when competition generates enough rent dissipation (reduces π^d sufficiently), then

$$\pi^m - \pi^d > \pi^d,$$

so that the incumbent is more likely to win the race and thereby persist as a monopoly.

However, it does not consider the effect of an increase in product market competition (i.e., of a reduction in the transport cost t) on π^m and π^d. Clearly, the entrant responds negatively to an increase in product market competition, as his post-entry profit π^d decreases when t decreases (this is the Schumpeterian effect emphasized earlier). On the other hand, the incumbent may respond positively to higher competition, insofar as π^d decreases more with competition than π^m does, so that the rent dissipation $\pi^m - \pi^d$ goes up when t goes down.

Much of the analysis in this book revolves around these two effects, first within a particular sector, and then across sectors with different technological characteristics, and their impact on the magnitude of cost or quality differences between incumbent and entrant. This brings us to a second important extension of the above models of price competition and entry.

The Importance of Vertical Differentiation   Let us go back to the circular model, but now suppose that some firms have higher unit costs than others. Thus firms are not only horizontally differentiated along the circle, but also vertically differentiated by their costs. In this case, as shown in Aghion and Schankerman 2003, more intense product market competition, modeled again as a reduction in the unit transport cost t, can enhance "innovations" through several channels that counteract the negative effect pointed out previously. First, by increasing the market share of low-cost firms at the expense of high-cost firms (this is referred to as the "election effect" of product market competition), more intense competition may end up encouraging entry by low-cost firms (especially if potential low-cost entrants are far less numerous than high-cost entrants). Second, and again because it increases the market share of low-cost firms relative to high-cost firms, more intense competition will induce high-cost firms to invest in "restructuring" in order to become low-cost firms themselves. Note that such an investment amounts to a quality-improving innovation that allows the high-cost firm to suffer less from more intense competition. This type of effect will also play an important role in subsequent chapters of this book.

1.1.3   The Endogenous Growth Paradigm

Main Idea   Reading around the literature more broadly, our explorer would find that the prediction that product market competition has an unambiguously negative effect on entry or innovation is shared by the models of endogenous technical change in growth theory (e.g., Romer 1990; Aghion and Howitt 1992; Grossman and Helpman 1991). In all of these models, an increase in product market competition, or in the rate of imitation, has a negative effect on productivity growth by

reducing the monopoly rents that reward new innovation. This discourages firms from engaging in R&D activities, thereby lowering the
innovation rate and therefore also the rate of long-run growth, which
in these models is proportional to the innovation rate. In the product
variety framework of Romer (1990), this property is directly inherited
from the Dixit-Stiglitz model upon which this model is built. But the
same effect is also at work in the Schumpeterian (or quality-ladder)
models of Aghion and Howitt (1992) and Grossman and Helpman
(1991). These two models predict that property right protection is
growth-enhancing, however, for exactly the same reason they also predict that competition policy is unambiguously detrimental to growth:
Patent protection protects monopoly rents from innovation, whereas
increased product market competition destroys these rents. Thus, if we
were to take these models at face value when making policy prescrip-
tions, we would never advocate that patent policy and antitrust be
pursued at the same time, at least not from the point of view of promoting dynamic efficiency.[5]

Here we present a simplified version of the Schumpeterian growth
model with quality-improving innovations. This serves as a basis for
the theoretical extensions we will present in later chapters of this book
and provide a framework in which the tension between theory and evidence can be reconciled.

A Benchmark Model of Innovation and Productivity Growth   Consider an economy with a final good, y, and a continuum of intermediate inputs indexed by $i \in [0,1]$. Time is discrete, indexed by
$t = 1, 2, \ldots, T$. One final good is produced competitively using a continuum of mass 1 of intermediate inputs according to the constant
returns to scale production function:

$$y_t = \int_0^1 A_t(i)^{1-\alpha} x_t(i)^{\alpha} \, di, \tag{1.3}$$

where each $x_t(i)$ is the flow of intermediate input i used at date t, and
$A_t(i)$ is a productivity variable that measures the quality of the input.
This variable will grow over time as a result of quality-improving
innovations. The final good is used in turn for consumption, research,
and production of the intermediate inputs. For notational simplicity,
we omit the arguement i except when it is necessary.

Each intermediate sector is monopolized by an incumbent producer
(the incumbent innovator in that sector) who can produce the leading-

edge version of input i at a constant marginal cost of one unit of the final good. Each individual producer lives for one period only and therefore maximizes short-run profits. But she faces a competitive fringe of imitators who can produce the same input at a constant marginal cost $\chi > 1$. The parameter χ is an inverse measure of the degree of product market competition or imitation in the economy: The higher is χ, the greater the innovators' market power and thus the lower the degree of competition.[6] The incumbent producer is forced to charge a limit price (in terms of the final good, our numeraire) equal to

$$p_t = \chi.$$

to prevent the fringe from stealing her market.

Because the final-good-producing sector is competitive, price is also equal to marginal productivity:

$$p_t = \partial y_t / \partial x_t(i) = \alpha (x_t(i)/A_t(i))^{\alpha-1}.$$

Equating the two expressions for the price, we get

$$x_t(i) = \left(\frac{\chi}{\alpha}\right)^{1/(\alpha-1)} A_t(i),$$

so that the equilibrium monopoly rent of the incumbent producer in sector i is equal to

$$\pi_t(i) = (p_t - 1)x_t(i) = \delta(\chi)A_t(i),$$

where

$$\delta(\chi) \equiv (\chi - 1)(\chi/\alpha)^{1/(\alpha-1)}.$$

Innovations in sector i at the beginning of period t result in an improved version of the corresponding intermediate input. Namely, an innovation at t multiplies the preexisting productivity parameter $A_{t-1}(i)$ by a factor $\gamma > 1$.

Innovations in turn result from research z. By incurring an effort cost

$$c_{ti}(z) = \frac{1}{2}A_{t-1}(i)z^2$$

at the beginning of the period, some individual in sector i can become the new "leading-edge" producer of the intermediate input with probability λz. The payoff to research in sector i is the prospect of the monopoly rent $\pi_t(i)$ if the research succeeds in producing an innovation.

Assuming that all individuals can imitate the current technology after one period, this implies that a non-innovating incumbent makes no current profit, and that the monopoly rent of an innovating producer lasts for one period only.

Assume the time period is short enough that we may ignore the possibility of more than one successful innovator in the same sector. Then

$$A_t(i) = \begin{cases} \gamma A_{t-1}(i) & \text{with probability } \lambda n \\ A_{t-1}(i) & \text{with probability } 1 - \lambda n \end{cases} \tag{1.4}$$

where n is the equilibrium R&D investment in any sector i. The average growth rate is then simply given by

$$g = E(\ln A_t(i) - \ln A_{t-1}(i)) = \lambda n \ln \gamma$$

in an equilibrium where productivity-adjusted research is a constant n.

Now, the optimal R&D investment is the one that maximizes expected profits minus costs, namely,

$$\max_z \left\{ \lambda z \pi_t(i) - \frac{1}{2} A_{t-1}(i) z^2 \right\},$$

with first-order condition

$$z = n = \lambda(\pi_t(i)/A_{t-1}(i))$$

$$= \lambda \gamma(\pi_t(i)/A_t(i)),$$

or equivalently,

$$n = \lambda \gamma (\chi - 1)(\chi/\alpha)^{1/(\alpha-1)}.$$

The corresponding average rate of productivity growth is simply

$$g = \lambda^2 \gamma (\chi - 1)(\chi/\alpha)^{1/(\alpha-1)} \ln \gamma.$$

In particular, productivity growth is decreasing with the degree of product market competition (or with the degree of imitation), as inversely measured by χ. Thus, as we stressed at the beginning of this section, patent protection (or, more generally, better protection of intellectual property rights) will enhance growth by increasing χ and therefore increasing potential rewards from innovation. However, pro-competition policies will tend to discourage innovation and growth by reducing χ, and thereby forcing incumbent innovators to charge a lower limit price.

Our observer may ask: How come we have a model with vertical innovation that nevertheless delivers the same prediction as the Salop and Dixit-Stiglitz models of horizontal differentiation and entry? At the same time, our reader will notice that, as in these other two models, innovation is always performed by outsiders, that is, by firms that make no profit before they innovate. This is in contrast with the preemption or restructuring models mentioned in the previous section. Also, note that all the researchers racing for the new innovation have access to the same R&D technology and they achieve the same productivity level if they successfully innovate, unlike high- versus low-cost entrants in the Aghion-Schankerman model. These considerations will suggest natural ways of extending the model so as to reconcile theory and empirics, as we will see in subsequent chapters.

1.2 The Evidence Contradicts the Theory

Before considering these theoretical extensions, our explorer may well decide to look to the empirical literature. Does it support the theory as laid out so far? Does it offer alternative avenues for investigation? The empirical literature linking product market competition to innovation and productivity growth predates the theoretical literature by several decades. Thus, our observer starts by looking back to the empirical literature of the mid-sixties, pioneered by Scherer, then jumps ahead (skipping volumes of work) twenty-five years to the more recent microecometric literature of the 1990s. And, as before, our explorer may spot a number of limitations to the various pieces of work, which upon closer examination might suggest ways to reconcile the theory and the evidence.

1.2.1 The Early Literature
A large early empirical literature, inspired by Schumpeter (1943), considered the cross-sectional relationship between innovation and firm size or market concentration.[7] Many studies found that larger firms (either measured by size or market share) were also more innovative (or spent more on R&D). Figure 1.2 shows this pattern, which is seen across a large number of datasets. Here we have graphed the average number of patents taken out at the U.S. Patent Office by firms listed on the London Stock Exchange. On the x-axis we have ranked firms by their size decile; the smallest firms are located in the first decile and

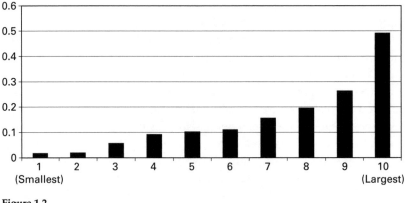

Figure 1.2
Patents by firm size decile

the largest firms in the tenth decile. The graph clearly shows that the
bulk of patenting is done by larger firms.[8]

Scherer's early empirical work[9] showed that there was a relationship
between firm patenting activity and firm size in the cross section. For
example, Scherer (1965a) used patents data on Fortune 500 firms in
1959 and regressed this on sales in 1955. He found a positive relationship. However, interestingly, he also found that when he allowed
for non-linearities these suggested a diminishing impact at larger
sizes. We will return to these non-linearities in later chapters. Scherer
(1965a) also investigated the relationship between four firm concentration indices and patenting activity and finds no significant results.
Summing up, he writes: "These findings among other things raise
doubts whether the big, monopolistic, conglomerate corporation is as
efficient an engine of technological change as disciples of Schumpeter
(including myself) have supposed it to be. Perhaps a bevy of fact-
mechanics can still rescue the Schumpeterian engine from disgrace,
but at present the outlook seems pessimistic" (1122).

In fact Scherer's pessimism was to be borne out. Over the next few
decades fact-mechanics (or econometricians as they are now called)
did not find evidence in favor of the Schumpeterian model; in fact,
quite the opposite was the case, as the empirical tide turned against
Schumpeter.

1.2.2 Methodological Challenges
Before skipping ahead to the recent microeconomic literature, our
explorer would do well to consider some of the methodological diffi-

culties faced by empirical researchers in this area. The early literature failed to reach robust conclusions principally because of a number of difficult methodological problems that were not dealt with, in large part due to lack of data.[10]

First, it turned out to be important to control for other firm and industry characteristics that affect innovation. This is because these other characteristics are correlated with firm size and market structure. For example, if we showed that firm size was positively associated with innovative output, but we had not controlled for firm age, then it could be the case that firm size is correlated with age (e.g., firms get bigger as they get older) and that firm age is also correlated with innovate output, and that this led to a spurious correlation between firm size and innovation. Unless we control for at least the main observable and unobservable characteristics, we can not be sure that we are really picking up the relationship between size and innovation.

Second, there is a problem of reverse causality. While firm size or market structure is likely to affect innovation, it is also the case that successful innovation affects market structure. Firms that are successful innovators will either have lower costs (so be able to sell at a lower price) or have superior quality goods, and in either case will gain market share.[11] To help deal with these first two difficulties, it is important to have panel data—repeated observations of the same individuals over time. Panel data in itself does not solve these problems. What is important is that there is exogenous variation in the degree of competition, for example, policy changes that make entry easier or less costly. If we are willing to assume that many of the firm characteristics that are correlated with market power are constant over time, then firm fixed effects can be used to control for them.[12] In addition, if we are willing to assume that market structure is predetermined (i.e., that feedback from innovation to market structure only affects future market shares, and the anticipation of innovation does not affect current market structure), then repeated observations of the same firm allow us to use lags of market structure.

Third, the relationship we are interested in is between product market competition and innovation, while the early literature largely focused on the relationship between firm size or market concentration and innovation. These may not be good measures of the degree of competition, and may in fact reflect other differences, for example, a firm's ability to access finance. Boone (2000) shows it is not always the case that an increase in competition reduces firm size, price cost margins, or concentration.[13] It can be difficult to obtain good measures of the degree of product market competition in an industry, and recent work has paid careful attention to this. Recent work has used a measure of rents, or the Lerner Index (see, e.g., Nickell 1996). This is the measure implied by much of the theory used in what follows and has several advantages over indicators such as market shares or a Herfindahl or concentration index. In order to measure any of those, it is necessary to have a definition of both the geographic and product boundaries of the market in which the firm operates. This is particularly important in applications where firms operate in international markets, so that traditional market concentration measures could be extremely misleading.[14]

A related, but somewhat separate point, is that it may be the case that firms with greater market share are more innovative (than those with lower market share), but if we are interested in aggregate (or industry) innovations then we have to weigh this against the fact that there will be fewer firms innovating in more concentrated markets, and thus industry innovation could go up or down.

Fourth, it can be difficult to measure innovative output. Measures that are commonly used at the firm level are R&D spending, patenting activity, innovation counts, and total factor productivity (TFP). However, each of these has its problems. R&D expenditure is an input, not an output. In addition, in many countries or time periods it has not been mandatory for firms to report it. For example, in the United Kingdom prior to 1990, it is frequently not reported. Patenting activity, innovation counts, and TFP are all output measures, but each has its own problems. Patents are a very heterogeneous measure of innovation.[15] One patent can represent a path-breaking new technology worth billions of dollars, while another can represent a fairly incremental improvement in an existing technology worth only tens of thousands of dollars. In order to get around this problem, many researchers use citation-weighted patents[16] or use stock market data to assign a value to a patent. Another problem with patents is that the propensity to patent, and the degree to which they provide protection of intellectual property rights, varies substantially from industry to industry. For example, patents are widely used in the pharmaceuticals industry, but rarely used in the computer software industry. Innovation counts have also been used. An example is the Science Policy Research Unit (SPRU) innovations dataset for the United Kingdom.[17] These type of data are laborious to collect and suffer from problems similar to those of patents in the sense that they are very heterogeneous in their value and it is difficult to obtain consistent measures, particularly over time. However, where available, they can provide a rich source of detailed information. The final measure, TFP, is a measure of technological progress (and thus implemented innovative activity), but it can be difficult to accurately measure because of the well-known problem that commonly used measures of TFP are themselves biased in the presence of imperfectly competitive product markets.[18]

After considering these difficulties, our intrepid explorer may well consider giving up and going home. However, a combination of improved data availability (and, in particular, the availability of firm-level panel data sets), better econometric methods and more computing power meant that many of these problems could be tackled by the mid-1990s.

1.2.3   The 1990s

Rather than survey all of the papers in this area, we have steered our explorer to two specific papers that directly addressed these issues—Nickell 1996 and Blundell, Griffith, and Van Reenen 1999.[19] These both use data on firms listed on the London Stock Exchange. The United Kingdom turned out to be a good place to study the relation between product market competition and innovation because there have been a large number of policy changes that led to (relatively) exogenous variation in the nature and magnitude of product market structures and competition. These included the large-scale privatizations of the 1980s and 1990s, reforms associated with EU integration, and the opening up of markets in numerous other ways.

Nickell (1996)   Nickell (1996) considered the link between market structure and both the level and growth rate in TFP.[20] Nickell's paper was the first to tackle these empirical issues head on. Using firm-level panel data, he was able to control for unobservable (correlated) characteristics that were constant over time. He developed and used better measures of product market competition including market share, concentration, import penetration, rents, and survey-based measures. The measure based on rents is particularly interesting as it is robust to a number of concerns about identifying the markets in which firms operate. Primarily, it does not require the econometrician to be able to define and observe the entire market(s) in which the firm operates, unlike alternative measures such as market share, Herfindahl, or concentration indices.

While Nickell's measure of TFP suffers from the bias mentioned previously (it is negatively correlated with the degree of product market competition), Nickell points out that this would only work against his findings—it would make it more likely to find evidence *supporting* the Schumpeterian hypothesis of competition being bad for innovation. Nickell provides convincing support for the idea that tougher competition in the product market is associated with higher growth rates in TFP—higher concentration and a higher level of rents are associated with lower growth rates of TFP.

Nickell estimates an augmented production function. The basic equation of interest (Nickell 1996, eq. (5)) is

$$\ln \frac{Y_{it}}{K_{it}} = \phi_1 \ln\left(\frac{Y_{it-1}}{K_{it}}\right) + \phi_2 \ln\left(\frac{L_{it}}{K_{it}}\right) + \phi_3 MS_{it-2}$$

$$+ t(\phi_4 SZ_i + \phi_5 RT_i + \phi_6 C_j + \phi_7 IMP_j) + X'_{it}\lambda + e_{it}, \tag{1.5}$$

where i indexes firms, Y is output, L is labor inputs, K is capital inputs, MS is firm market share, t is a time trend, SZ is firm size, RT is the level of rents earned by the firm (normalized by value-added), C is an industry-level concentration ratio (market share of the top five firms), IMP is industry import penetration, and X is a vector of other variables including firm and time effects (to capture unobservable characteristics of the firm that may be correlated with the variables of interest).

Notice that this specification implies that market share, in contrast to other competition measures in equation (1.5), affects the firm's *level* of TFP. The other measures (SZ_i, RT_i, C_j, IMP_j) are measured at the cross-sectional level (they are not time-varying) and are multiplied by t, which represents a time trend. This means that they are modeled as affecting the growth rate of TFP. When equation (1.5) is differenced, to remove firm-level unobservable characteristics, the model becomes

$$\Delta \ln \frac{Y_{it}}{K_{it}} = \phi_1 \Delta \ln\left(\frac{Y_{it-1}}{K_{it}}\right) + \phi_2 \Delta \ln\left(\frac{L_{it}}{K_{it}}\right) + \phi_3 \Delta MS_{it-2}$$

$$+ \phi_4 SZ_i + \phi_5 RT_i + \phi_6 C_j + \phi_7 IMP_j + \Delta X'_{it}\lambda + \Delta e_{it},$$

where Δ represents the one-year difference (e.g., $\Delta x_{it} = x_{it} - x_{it-1}$). This makes it clear that it is the levels of SZ_i, RT_i, C_j, and IMP_j that affect the growth rate of TFP. Our interpretation of the difference between an effect on the level of innovation versus the growth rate is something we return to in the next chapter. For now it suffices to note that the main results of interest to us here in Nickell's (1996) paper are those on the growth rate of TFP.

The estimates of the coefficients of interest in Nickell's basic specification all indicate that increased competition is associated with a higher level and faster growth rates of TFP. Column (1) of table 1 in Nickell 1996 suggests that the coefficient on market share (ϕ_3) was -3.49 (and was statistically significant with a t-statistic of 2.1), suggesting that firms with lower market share had higher *levels* of TFP. The coefficients on size (ϕ_4) and imports (ϕ_7) were positive, but not statistically significant. The coefficient on rents (ϕ_5), which is a measure of the degree of competition the firm faces in the product market (the higher a firm's rents, the less competitive the market), is -0.13 (and was statistically significant with a t-statistic of 2.9), suggesting that firms in more competitive markets had higher growth rates of TFP.

What economic interpretation do we put on these estimates? Nickell reports the distribution of rents as being zero at the twentieth percentile and 0.29 at the eightieth percentile. Looking at a very similar data set, we can see that the mean and median are around 0.20. Combining this with the estimated coefficient on RT_i of -0.13, we get that increasing competition by going from the eightieth percentile in the distribution of rents to the twentieth (reducing rents means increasing competition) increases TFP growth by around 3.8 percentage points. This is a large and economically significant effect. Moving from the median to the twentieth percentile would be associated with an increase in TFP growth of around 1.2 percentage points.

The impact of competition on innovation, as measured by TFP, is illustrated in figure 1.3. This figure plots the values of $-0.13*RT_i$, normalized to zero at the lowest level of competition. The far right hand of the x-axis (where $(1 - RT) = 1$) represents perfect competition (zero rents), while the far left-hand end of the x-axis represents a low level of competition (rents of 30 percent).

The coefficient on industry concentration (ϕ_6) was -0.12 (and was statistically significant with a t-statistic of 2.1). Performing a similar exercise, we find that the industry concentration ratio at the twentieth percentile is 0.25 (the top five firms make up 25 percent of total output) and at the eightieth is 0.60 (the top five firms account for 60 percent of output), with a mean of 0.41 and median of 0.43. If an industry moves

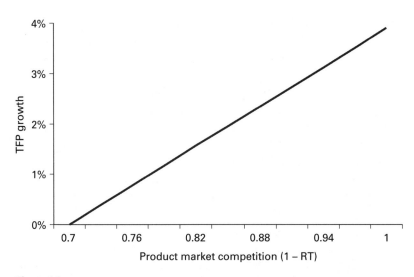

Figure 1.3
Relationship between product market competition and total factor productivity implied by Nickell 1996 results

from being very concentrated (at the eightieth percentile) to being fairly unconcentrated (at the twentieth percentile), ceteris paribus, this will be associated with an increase in TFP growth of 4.2 percentage points. Again, this is a large impact.

Another way to look at the economic importance of these estimates is to look at how much of TFP growth is explained by differences in competition. Nickell creates an index of competition that equals

$$\phi_5 RT_i + \phi_6 C_j. \tag{1.6}$$

Nickell reports the value of this across industries and they are substantial, as shown in table 1.1.[21] This shows the differences that arise in average industry growth rates due to differences in the level of competition across these industries, holding everything else constant. For example, TFP growth in electrical engineering was 2.4 percentage points lower, on average, due to low levels of competition, while mechanical engineering experienced TFP growth that was around 1 percentage point higher due to relatively higher levels of competition.

Blundell, Griffith, and Van Reenen (1999)   Another micro study by Blundell, Griffith, and Van Reenen (1999), also uses U.K. firm-level panel data, but rather than using TFP it uses the SPRU innovation

Table 1.1
Percentage point TFP growth rate differentials generated by differences in competition

Food, drink, and tobacco	−.2	Metal goods (other)	.8
Chemicals	−.8	Textiles	.9
Metal manufacture	−1.7	Clothing and footwear	1.0
Mechanical engineering	1.0	Bricks, pottery, and glass	2.0
Instrument engineering	−.6	Timber and furniture	1.6
Electrical engineering	−2.4	Paper, printing, and publishing	1.9
Vehicles	−1.3	Other manufacturing	−2.2

Source: Nickell 1996, table 3.
Note: These are differentials from the unweighted mean.

count to measure innovative output.[22] Competition is measured using market share, concentration, and import penetration. The main contribution of this paper was to embed the empirical work in a clear theoretical framework in order to address the question of *why* market dominance enables firms to be more innovative. There were two main interpretations of Schumpeter's work emphasized in the literature. The first said that financial market failures meant that firms had to rely on their own internal sources of funds in order to finance innovation, and that larger firms had deeper pockets and were thus better able to do this. The second focused on the incentive effects of market power as highlighted, for example, by Gilbert and Newbery (1982), who argued that monopolists will tend to innovate more than entrants because of the reduction in total industry profits that the incumbent suffers due to entry. In contradiction to this is the displacement effect emphasized by, for example, Reinganum (1983), whereby a monopolist is less keen on innovating because this will replace some of the current stream of rents, while the entrant does not suffer from such disincentives.

Blundell, Griffith, and Van Reenen (1999) also tackle a number of the econometric issues, incorporating dynamics and controlling for firm fixed effects in a nonlinear model. The main equations estimated are an innovation equation

$$I_{it} = \exp(\alpha_1 MS_{it-1} + \alpha_2 SZ_{it-1} + \alpha_3 C_{jt-1} + \alpha_4 IMP_{jt-1} + X'_{it}\lambda + u_{it}) \quad (1.7)$$

and a market value equation

$$\ln V_{it} = \alpha_5 \ln K_{it} + \alpha_6 G/K_{it} + \alpha_7 MS_{it} + \alpha_8(G/K_{it})MS_{it} + X'_{it}\lambda' + \varepsilon_{it}, \quad (1.8)$$

where I is a count of innovation from the SPRU dataset, V is firm market value on the London Stock Exchange, and G is stock of

innovations; as in the previous case, i indexes firm, MS is firm market
share, SZ is firm size, C is an industry-level concentration ratio (market
share of the top five firms), IMP is industry import penetration, K is
tangible capital, and X is a vector of other variables including firm and
time effects.

Blundell, Griffith, and Van Reenen's results showed that less
competitive industries (those with higher concentration levels and
lower imports) had fewer aggregate innovation, as shown in table 1.2.
Column 1 shows the estimates from a regression of the form shown
in equation (2.7), while columns (2)–(6) extend this to alternative dynamic specifications. Focusing on columns (2) and (3), which represent
alternative dynamic specifications, we see that the coefficient on the
concentration ratio (α_3) is negative and significant and the coefficient
on market share (α_1) is positive and significant. This suggests that
tougher competition (a lower concentration ratio) is associated with
higher levels of innovation, even though within industries it was the
higher market share firms that innovated most frequently.

While the point estimates on the market share coefficient differ
across columns (2) and (3) the economic interpretation is also not the
same, because of the different dynamic specifications. In fact, the two
estimates suggest very similar short-run impacts and elasticities. The
short-run impact of market share on innovation is 0.15 in column (2)
and 0.16 in column (3), and the elasticity of innovation with respect to
market share, evaluated at the mean market share, is 0.08 in column (2)
and 0.10 in column (3).

One of the contributions of Blundell, Griffith, and Van Reenen is that
considering, on the one hand, the relationship between market structure and innovation, and, on the other hand, the impact that market
structure has on the relationship between innovation and market value
enables the authors to distinguish between the two reasons for seeing a
positive correlation between market share and innovation—financial
constraints or incentive effects. In column (4) of table 1.2, Blundell,
Griffith, and Van Reenen included a measure of free cash flow and
showed that market share was not simply picking up the effect of
greater liquidity in larger firms. Estimates of equation (1.8), shown in
table 1.3, examine this issue further. The econometric results shown
there lend support to the Gilbert and Newbery preemption effect
(1982) discussed in section 1.1.2. The coefficient on the interaction between market share and firms' knowledge capital stock (α_8) was posi-

Table 1.2
The innovation equation estimates

	(1)	(2)	(3)	(4)	(5)	(6)
G_{-1}	—	—	0.123	0.122	0.156	−0.086
			0.052	*0.052*	*0.037*	*0.352*
$\ln(G_{-1})$	—	0.331	—	—	—	—
		0.081				
G_{-1} dum	—	0.540	—	—	—	—
		0.750				
MS_{-1}	4.318	1.336	2.534	2.568	3.207	3.739
	0.988	*0.451*	*0.713*	*0.699*	*1.028*	*3.278*
$Conc_{-1}$	−1.967	−1.498	−2.198	−2.190	−1.759	−6.499
	0.936	*0.676*	*0.976*	*0.896*	*1.135*	*11.111*
$Imports_{-1}$	1.214	0.987	1.258	1.316	1.597	0.841
	0.925	*0.806*	*1.118*	*1.312*	*1.254*	*2.941*
K_{-1}	0.894	0.124	0.208	0.200	0.060	0.036
	0.228	*0.122*	*0.181*	*0.191*	*0.244*	*0.494*
$Cash_{-1}$	—	—	—	−0.207	—	—
				0.534		
$G\text{-}Prod_{-1}$	−0.282	−0.466	−0.422	−0.416	−0.133	−0.768
	0.567	*0.384*	*0.547*	*0.548*	*0.629*	*3.612*
$G\text{-}User_{-1}$	4.917	2.562	3.278	3.288	2.299	1.662
	1.740	*1.381*	*1.900*	*1.920*	*2.174*	*2.596*
$\ln(G_0)$	—	0.452	0.838	0.829	0.862	—
		0.106	*0.114*	*0.114*	*0.129*	
G_0 dum	—	0.696	1.825	1.660	2.062	—
		0.793	*0.739*	*0.750*	*0.862*	
1973–1974	−0.300	−0.432	−0.957	−0.926	—	—
	0.153	*0.162*	*0.494*	*0.478*		
1980–1982	−0.993	−0.676	−0.934	−0.959	—	—
	0.209	*0.252*	*0.616*	*0.614*		
Constant	−2.956	−0.195	−0.327	−0.326	—	—
	0.588	*0.408*	*0.689*	*0.698*		
Time dummies	no	no	no	no	yes	yes
Observations	3511	3511	3511	3511	3511	3211
Time period	1972–1982	1972–1982	1972–1982	1972–1982	1972–1982	1972–1981
v_1	1.210	−0.270	−0.474	−0.472	−0.059	
v_2	2.980	0.271	−0.573	−0.572	−0.913	

Source: Blundell, Griffith, and Van Reenen 1999, table 4.1.
Notes: Standard errors are in italics and allow for general heteroskedasticity and autocorrelation. Dummy variables for GEC and ICI are included in all columns except (6). In columns (2)–(5) instruments include a single lag of each variable and the initial value of firm level variables (MS and K). v_1 and v_2 are the standard serial correlation statistics from Arellano and Bond (1991) distributed $N(0,1)$ under the null of no serial correlation. In column (6) instruments are lags of all variables.

Table 1.3
Market value in levels

	ln(V) (1)	ln(V) (2)	ln(V) (3)	ln(V) (4)	ln(V/K) (5)	ln(V/K) (6)	ln(V/K) (7)
ln(K)	0.688 *0.016*	1.098 *0.061*	1.095 *0.061*	1.088 *0.058*	—	—	—
G/K	1.928 *0.933*	2.064 *0.970*	1.421 *0.947*	1.615 *0.923*	1.582 *0.921*	1.840 *0.885*	4.370 *1.852*
MS	0.600 *0.144*	0.341 *0.380*	0.075 *0.350*	0.007 *0.329*	0.068 *0.327*	0.277 *0.327*	-0.001 *0.671*
$MS * (G/K)$[a]	—	—	1.588 *0.404*	1.733 *0.402*	1.745 *0.403*	1.767 *0.376*	1.715 *0.952*
Conc	—	—	—	0.374 *0.082*	0.379 *0.082*	0.385 *0.082*	0.441 *0.211*
Imports	—	—	—	-0.316 *0.099*	-0.319 *0.099*	-0.315 *0.099*	-0.321 *0.265*
Union	—	—	—	-0.260 *0.113*	-0.259 *0.113*	-0.264 *0.113*	-0.267 *0.271*
G-User	—	—	—	-0.345 *0.222*	-0.331 *0.223*	-0.357 *0.223*	-0.543 *0.500*
G-Prod	—	—	—	0.255 *0.062*	0.252 *0.062*	0.260 *0.062*	0.331 *0.136*
$\ln(V_0)$	—	0.151 *0.014*	0.152 *0.014*	0.141 *0.014*	0.141 *0.014*	0.142 *0.014*	0.144 *0.036*
G_0	—	0.145 *0.040*	0.004 *0.049*	-0.030 *0.056*	-0.029 *0.048*	-0.030 *0.047*	-0.026 *0.120*
G_0 dum	—	-0.182 *0.029*	-0.184 *0.028*	-0.181 *0.028*	-0.179 *0.028*	-0.184 *0.028*	-0.214 *0.069*

	(1)	(2)	(3)	(4)	(5)	(6)	(7)
$\ln(K_0)$	—	-0.413	-0.406	-0.408	-0.333	-0.335	-0.331
		0.059	*0.059*	*0.057*	*0.015*	*0.015*	*0.041*
MS_0	—	-0.491	-0.264	-0.031	-0.089	-0.305	-0.033
		0.408	*0.365*	*0.343*	*0.342*	*0.342*	*0.720*
Sargan (df)	—	—	—	—	—	325 (220)	207 (192)
p-value	—	—	—	—	—	0.000	0.216
Observations	3511	3511	3511	3511	3511	3511	3211
Years	1972–1982	1972–1982	1972–1982	1972–1982	1972–1982	1972–1982	1973–1982
v_1	10.21	11.03	10.98	11.16	11.11	11.00	9.82
v_2	9.36	10.19	10.13	10.27	10.19	9.97	8.16
$R^2(P - S)$	0.842	0.862	0.863	0.863	0.389		

Source: Blundell, Griffith, and Van Reenen 1999, table 4.2.

Notes: A full set of time dummies, a dummy for the chemical sector, ln (inventories) are included as additional controls in all specifications. Initial stock of log (inventories) is included in columns (2)–(7). Standard errors are in italics and allow for arbitrary heteroskedasticity. All industry-level variables are assumed exogenous. Instruments for firm-level variables (X_i) are columns X_{t-1} in (1)–(5), X_{t-1} to X_{t-7} in column (6), and ΔX_{t-1} to ΔX_{t-7} (except the interaction) in column (7). The Sargan test is distributed χ^2 under the null of instrument validity. $R^2(P - S)$ are calculated as in Pesaran and Smith 1995.

[a] Coefficients and standard errors divided by 100.

tive and statistically significant. This suggests that higher market share firms get a bigger payoff from an innovation, giving them a greater incentive to preemptively innovate.

In a slightly different form of the same specification, Blundell, Griffith, and Van Reenen (1999) estimate that an innovation is worth on average around £2m. This estimate is in line with others in the literature; for example, Geroski, Machin, and Van Reenen (1993) estimate a similar impact using data on profitability.

1.3 Conclusion

Not only the informal thinking of many economists, but also the empirical evidence of the mid-nineties, seemed to contradict the basic theoretical prediction that product market competition is detrimental to innovation and growth. As Nickell (1996) summarizes, "this general belief in the efficacy of competition exists despite the fact that it is not supported either by any strong theoretical foundations or by a large corpus of hard empirical evidence in its favor" (725).

So the theoretical work and empirical evidence were at odds. The empirical literature suggested that more competitive market structures were associated with greater innovative output, an idea that had much support in policy circles. However, the empirical models were missing something—in particular, work so far (excepting Scherer's early work) had only looked for linear effects. Our knowledge that, for example, patent protection (the granting of a time-limited monopoly to a firm) was good for innovation suggested that, at least over some ranges, less competition could be conducive to innovation. But this was not being captured in the empirical work.

There was also a need to reconsider the theoretical models that suggested that more competitive market structures had an unambiguously negative effect on innovation and productivity growth. These models were missing something too, including the possibility that innovations, particularly vertical innovations, could be made by incumbent firms in order to preempt or escape competition and entry.

In the following chapters, our explorer digs into these cracks in the theories and empirical studies on competition and growth and finds that harmony can be restored. Before doing that, however, we return in the next chapter to the common wisdom that competition increases productive efficiency.

2   Revisiting Common Wisdom

Our intrepid explorer will most likely remain skeptical of the existing theory. It seems that common wisdom, whereby competition should foster efficiency and productivity growth by forcing firms to innovate constantly in order to avoid bankruptcy, and the empirics line up against it.

A natural step forward should thus be for our explorer to look for models that formalize this "Darwinian" effect of competition and confront them with empirical evidence. Here the United Kingdom and the EU provide not only useful evidence but also the experience of firms from post-communist transition economies. These offer a perfect laboratory in which to test the idea that hard budget constraints and market competition combined may act as an engine of growth in a world dominated by inefficient firms.

One distinction that we alluded to in the last chapter, but that we should emphasize here, is whether we are considering the impact of competition on the *level* of efficiency or the level of TFP, or on the *growth rate*, which is more closely aligned with innovation. There is little disagreement over the fact that market power leads to allocative inefficiency—prices do not reflect costs and therefore goods are not allocated optimally. In addition, there is now little disagreement that competition promotes productive efficiency. In particular, the idea, formalized first by Hart (1983), that competition increases productivity by acting as a incentive scheme to ensure that managers (and workers) do not buy themselves a "quiet life" (i.e., slack or consume leisure on the job) is now firmly entrenched in economics and in common beliefs. However, stated as such, these are both level effects. The question then is: Can these same effects also capture the impact of competition on innovation and growth, and thereby explain the positive correlations found in the previous chapter?

To answer this question, our explorer will first need to be introduced to the "satisficing" managers of Hart (1983), who seek a quiet life subject to survival. This can be put into the growth model of the previous chapter, and she can look under which conditions competition, combined with the threat of bankruptcy, can force managers to innovate constantly and thereby achieve a higher rate of growth. She will then want to look for evidence confronting the predictions of this extended model with data on firms that are most likely to experience managerial slack and also bankruptcy threats. Particularly good candidates in this respect are firms with hard-budget constraints that experience a high degree of separation between ownership and management: for example, those firms in transition economies that used to be state-owned and are subsequently privatized and subject to full market competition with new private entrants.

While our observer will find empirical support for the idea that competition improves the level of efficiency in those firms most likely to suffer from slack, unfortunately she will find mixed evidence that it increases growth or that it affects these firms more than profit-maximizing firms. At this point our observer will have found little help from common wisdom to explain the empirical findings of the previous chapter and to reconcile it with the theory. In order to help her we may find some hints by looking back at the theoretical IO literature, and in particular the preemption models (briefly discussed in chapter 1). In this chapter we discuss recent work that extends the endogenous growth model of the previous chapter in order to derive testable predictions that are consistent with the data.

2.1 Competition as a Slack-Reducing Device

2.1.1 Competition as an Incentive Scheme
Hart (1983) formalized the notion that product market competition enhances productive efficiency in the context of a model of monopolistic competition. More specifically, Hart considers an economic environment where firms are subject to "agency problems" due to the non-observability of both managerial effort *and* managerial performance (e.g., managers can manipulate profits over time). In standard models of moral hazard (e.g., Holmstrom 1979), agents' efforts are not observable but output performance is observable, so that the firm's owner (the principal) can design a wage schedule contingent upon the agent's performance in order to provide effort incentives to the agent

(under the assumption that effort and performance are positively correlated). When profits or other measures of performance are not observable, monetary incentive schemes are no longer feasible and one has to look for alternatives. One alternative, analyzed by Holmstrom (1982), is to rely on career concerns and the market for managers. Another alternative, analyzed by Hart, is to rely on product market competition together with a manager's fear of losing her job as a result of the firm going bankrupt.

More formally, Hart assumes that a positive fraction of firms are non-profit-maximizing in the sense that they are run by managers who do not respond to monetary incentives. He assumes instead that, in those firms, managers obtain a utility of $-\infty$ if they receive less than some minimum income $\bar{I}$, and a fixed utility U_0 if they receive an income at least equal to $\bar{I}$. Some authors use the term *satisficing* when they refer to managers with such preferences. The main result in Hart 1983 is that in such an environment it may be (weakly) optimal for the owner of a non-profit-maximizing firm to choose an incentive scheme whereby her manager is paid $\bar{I}$ as long as the firm's profit remains greater than some lower bound π_0, and zero otherwise. One can easily reinterpret this contracting situation as one where managers enjoy private benefits of control, U_0, as long as the firm remains in business, but have a negative utility of becoming unemployed. In this case, debt financing will amount to imposing the same kind of incentive scheme upon managers, namely, through the creditors' threat of closing down the firm if profits are not sufficiently high for their loans to be repaid.

How does product market competition come into play? The answer is very simple. Suppose some exogenous change—say, in demand conditions—occurs, which induces profit-maximizing firms to innovate in order to reduce costs. These firms will react to their rivals' prices with a lower price in order to increase their market share. But this in turn will push all equilibrium prices downward, which in turn will induce non-profit-maximizing firms also to reduce costs so as to preserve their market share and thereby keep their profit flow above the bankruptcy threshold. Thus, even though relative performance schemes may not be feasible due to the non-observability of firms' revenues, Hart observes that the market mechanism makes actions and utilities of different managers interdependent via prices. Competition then acts as an incentive scheme to induce even non-profit-maximizing firms to reduce slack and improve their management methods. Thus *competition increases productive efficiency in firms subject to agency problems.*

In the next subsection we reformulate this idea in the context of the endogenous growth framework outlined in chapter 2. But before we do so, an important remark is in order. Scharfstein (1988), and more recently Schmidt (1997), have argued that the effect of product market competition on managerial incentives becomes ambiguous when managers respond to monetary incentives. In this case an increase in product market competition has two opposite effects on managerial incentives. On the one hand, it increases the threat of bankruptcy for firms that do not reduce costs in response to cost cutting by competitors. On the other hand, it reduces equilibrium profits and, therefore, the extent to which high-powered monetary incentives can be used to reward good performance by managers.

2.1.2   Competition and Growth in an Economy with Satisficing Managers

Aghion, Dewatripont, and Rey (1999) embed the agency model of Hart in an endogenous growth framework and show that competition should also have a positive effect on innovation and growth. In addition, they show that competition and a hard budget constraint are complementary. Consider the same economy as in chapter 1, where one final good is produced from a continuum of intermediate inputs according to

$$y_t = \int_0^1 A_t(i)^{1-\alpha} x_t(i)^\alpha \, di,$$

where each $x_t(i)$ is the flow of intermediate input i used at date t, and $A_t(i)$ is a productivity variable that measures the quality of the input. As in chapter 1, intermediate goods are produced using the final good as capital according to a one-for-one technology, and each intermediate good producer faces a competitive fringe of firms that can produce one unit of the same intermediate good using χ units of the final good, where $1 < \chi < (1/\alpha)$. χ is an (inverse) measure of product market competition.

Thus in equilibrium, as before, the innovator is forced to charge a limit price equal to

$$p_t(i) = \chi = \partial y_t / \partial x_t(i) = \alpha(x_t / A_t(i))^{\alpha-1};$$

hence, the equilibrium monopoly rent is

$$\pi_t(i) = (p_t(i) - 1)x_t(i) = (\chi - 1)x_t(i),$$

or equivalently

$$\pi_t(i) = \delta(\chi)A_t(i),$$

where

$$\delta(\chi) \equiv (\chi - 1)(\chi/\alpha)^{1/(\alpha-1)}.$$

Now, let us make two changes with respect to the model in chapter 1. First, we want to introduce the possibility of bankruptcy, and for that purpose we assume the existence of a fixed cost of production, which grows at the economy-wide growth rate. For notational simplicity, we take this cost to be equal to

$$k_t = \kappa A_{t-1}.$$

Second, we assume that individual producers decide not on the frequency (which we fix at one) but rather on the size γ of the productivity improvement. Suppose the effort cost to achieve a productivity improvement of size γ is

$$d(\gamma) = \frac{1}{2}\gamma^2 A_{t-1}.$$

Third, we consider two kinds of firms: profit-maximizing firms where managers choose γ to maximize profits minus effort cost, and non-profit-maximizing firms where managers are mainly concerned with preserving their private benefits of control, which in turn requires that profits net of the fixed cost of production remain positive in order to avoid bankruptcy. We now analyze how an increase in product market competition (i.e., a reduction in χ) affects the size of innovations in profit- and non-profit-maximizing (or satisficing) firms respectively.

1. *Profit-maximizing firms:* A profit-maximizing manager will choose γ to solve

$$\max_{\gamma}\left\{\delta(\chi)\gamma A_{t-1} - \frac{1}{2}\gamma^2 A_{t-1}\right\};$$

hence, by the first-order condition

$$\gamma^{pm} = \delta(\chi). \tag{2.1}$$

In particular, an increase in product market competition (a reduction in χ) *reduces* the optimal size of innovation γ^{pm}, which in turn leads to a lower rate of productivity growth, which is now equal to

$$g = 1. \ln \gamma^{pm} = \ln \delta(\chi). \tag{2.2}$$

2. *Non-profit-maximizing firms:* A satisficing manager will choose the minimum value of γ that guarantees at least zero *net* profits; in other words, she will choose the smallest value of γ that satisfies the equation

$$\delta(\chi)\gamma A_{t-1} = \kappa A_{t-1},$$

or equivalently,

$$\gamma^{npm} = \frac{\kappa}{\delta(\chi)}. \tag{2.3}$$

In particular, an increase in product market competition (a reduction in χ) *increases* the size of innovation γ^{npm}, which in turn leads to a higher rate of productivity growth g. Thus, as in Hart 1983, competition acts as an incentive scheme for managers to invest more in quality improvements, but only in firms where a principal-agent problem arises, so that the firm is non-profit-maximizing.

An interesting extension of our analysis in this section is to introduce debt financing and to look at how it interacts with product market competition. Suppose that the firm's manager faces a debt repayment obligation d_t, where

$$d_t = dA_{t-1}.$$

Then the innovation size chosen by a satisficing manager is simply equal to

$$\gamma^{npm} = \frac{\kappa + d}{\delta(\chi)},$$

which in turn shows that an increase in d has the same effect as a reduction in χ. In addition, the two instruments are *complementary* in the sense that the higher the d, the stronger the effect of an increase in product market competition (PMC) on innovation size and productivity growth. More formally,

$$\frac{\partial^2 \gamma^{npm}}{\partial d \partial \chi} > 0.$$

2.1.3   Main Theoretical Predictions
Our observer has now completed her theoretical exploration of the popular idea that competition may enhance the level and growth rate of productivity by reducing managerial slack and forcing managers to respond more promptly to cost reductions by other firms. She leaves theoryland with three main predictions to guide her search for empirical evidence on competition, efficiency, and growth in profit- and non-profit-maximizing firms.

• *Prediction 1:* PMC enhances productivity *levels* to a larger extent in satisficing firms—that is, firms with higher slack or a higher degree of separation between ownership and management—than in profit-maximizing firms.

• *Prediction 2:* An increase in PMC should have a more positive effect on productivity *growth* in satisficing firms than in profit-maximizing ones.

• *Prediction 3:* Debt financing and PMC are *complementary instruments* in an economy dominated by satisficing managers, in the sense that the higher the firm's debt repayment obligation, the more positive the effect of PMC on productivity growth.

2.2   Empirical Evidence

So once again our intrepid explorer turns to the empirical evidence: Does competition act as an incentive scheme, and does the observed impact of competition on productivity levels and productivity growth confirm any or all of the three predictions formulated previously? We consider each prediction in turn to help guide our explorer on her brief tour of the available empirical literature.

2.2.1   The Level Effect of Prediction 1
Here our explorer finds a wealth of evidence showing that more intense product market competition is associated with higher efficiency levels and less slack. Numerous approaches have been taken to test this prediction.

The first looked at the impact of changes in ownership (e.g., from state-owned public enterprises to privately owned firms) and deregulation on efficiency levels.[23] Most studies in this vein found that privatization, and more specifically the introduction of competition, is associated with improvements in efficiency.

A second strand used information on firms' outstanding debt or debt payments as a measure of the toughness of the budget constraint. Higher debt is taken as an indicator of a tougher budget constraint. The problem that researchers face is that (1) ex post debt might not be a very good measure of the firm's budget constrant, for example, firms that face lower borrowing costs will borrow more, while those facing higher borrowing costs will borrow less, and (2) debt is likely to be endogenous, for example, high growth firms are likely to face lower borrowing costs and so borrow more. Both of these will make it less likely that we will find the predicted relationship. Two papers from this literature are of particular interest to us here.

The first, Nickell and Nicolitsas 1999, looks at whether firms that are faced with financial pressure respond by increasing their efforts to raise productivity. The idea that they are interested in is whether, when financial pressure increases, managers work harder to minimize bankruptcy risks. Managers can do this by reducing employment, holding back on pay increases, or looking for productivity improvements.

The findings in this paper suggest that increasing financial pressure has a large negative effect on employment, a small negative effect on wage increases, and a small positive effect on the level of productivity. Nickell and Nicolitsas (1999) estimate a model of the form discussed in section 1.2.3 with the ratio of interest payments to cash flow additionally entered in levels (so this effects the level of TFP). They report that identification of the effects comes from "the substantial exogenous shifts in interest rates which have been instituted by government policy over the sample period" (1443). Nickell and Nicolitsas's findings suggest a statistically signficant but very small impact of increased financial pressure on the level of TFP. Another paper that reaches similar conclusions is Jagannathan and Srivivasan 1999, using data on U.S. stock market–listed firms. Its authors look at whether firms that operate in less competitive markets are more likely to use free cash flow to reduce leverage and engage in less productive activities when compared to firms in more competitive markets. This is interpreted as managers in less competitive industries buying themselves a quiet life.

A second and related paper, Nickell, Nicolitsas, and Patterson 2001 looks at whether firms reorganize work and bring in new management practices more often in bad times than in good times. The idea is that when demand is low workers and managers have more free time, they face a greater threat of bankruptcy, leading them to use this time to avoid the possibility of bankruptcy. Nickell, Nicolitsas, and Patterson have information on a large number of managerial practices. They look at whether firm performance (with a two-year lag) affects the probability that a firm will adopt these managerial practices. The empirical results suggest that firms tend to remove restrictive workplace practices and introduce new technology more frequently when performance is worsening than when it is improving. Worsening performance is measured by a fall in market share or a fall in profits per capita. Firms with a higher debt burden are less likely to introduce new management practices. Firms tend to become more centralized when they face a higher bankruptcy threat.

A third strand of the literature uses information on executive compensation schemes. An example from this literature is the paper by Aggerwal and Sandwick (1999), who look at the relationship between executive compensation packages (in particular, what portion of compensation is linked to own firm performance and what portion is linked to rival firm performance) and the degree of competition. They find that, as competition increases, firms are less likely to link executive pay to their own firm's performance. This is because competition acts as an incentive scheme, and therefore allows the owners to improve managerial incentives while providing them with better insurance, which in turn they achieve through reducing the power of monetary incentives.

This broad range of empirical evidence supports Hart's model: There is evidence that managers attempt to buy themselves a quiet life, that they put more effort into efficiency-improving activities when the threat of bankruptcy is greater, and that firms choose contracts that link executives' performance to other firms when markets are less competitive.

2.2.2 The Growth Effect of Prediction 2

But our explorer's real interest lies in understanding the links between product market competition and productivity *growth*, and in particular the effect on satisficing firms relative to profit-maximizing ones. Here, the evidence is less overwhelming.

As outlined in chapter 1, there is substantial evidence that product market competition is positively associated with productivity growth and innovation. However, our interest is whether this effect is particularly stronger for "satisficing" firms. A point to make here is that both Nickell (1996) and Blundell, Griffith, and Van Reenen (1999) were looking only at firms listed on the London Stock Exchange, who

Table 2.1
Impact of shareholder control and competition on productivity growth (1985–1994)

| Independent variables | Dependent variable: Δy_{it} | | |
	1	2	3
	SC95	SC95	SC90
Δy_{it-1}	0.16	0.16	0.17
	(2.3)	(2.4)	(2.5)
Δn_{it}	0.57	0.57	0.57
	(3.5)	(3.5)	(3.5)
Δk_{it}	0.27	0.27	0.26
$\Delta(H_{0jt}/H_{njt})$	1.03	1.03	1.02
	(2.6)	(2.6)	(2.5)
$10^{-3}\Delta(H_{0jt}/H_{njt})^{-1}$	2.14	2.15	2.13
	(2.9)	(2.9)	(2.9)
$\Delta mksh_{it-2}$	−0.67	−0.68	−0.61
	(2.0)	(2.0)	(1.9)
$conc_j.$	−0.024	−0.029	−0.06
	(0.5)	(0.6)	(1.1)
$imp_j.$	0.22	0.23	0.27
	(1.6)	(1.6)	(1.8)
$10^{-2}size_i$	−0.15	−0.097	−0.078
	(0.5)	(0.3)	(0.3)
$rent_{1i}$	−0.086	−0.091	−0.099
	(2.6)	(2.7)	(2.8)
SC_{i1}	0.032	−0.091	−0.011
	(2.2)	(1.7)	(1.1)
SC_{i2}	−0.006		−0.004
	(0.4)		(0.3)
SC_{i3}	−0.017	−0.016	0.003
	(2.1)	(2.0)	(0.3)
$SC_{i1} \times rent_{1i}$		0.995	0.39
		(2.2)	(3.3)
Serial correlation $[N(0,1)]$	−1.77	−1.75	−1.75
Instrument validity	$\chi^2(56) = 62.3$	$\chi^2(56) = 62.6$	$\chi^2(56) = 62.6$
se	0.066	0.066	0.066
Time dummies	✓	✓	✓
N	125	125	125
NT	854	854	854

Source: Nickell, Nicolitsas, and Dryden 1997, table 2.
Notes:
(i) $y = \ln(\text{real sales})$, $n = \ln(\text{employment})$, $k = \ln(\text{capital stock})$, $H_0 = $ industry overtime hours, $H_n = $ industry standard hours, $mksh = $ market share, $conc = $ average industry concentration ratio, $imp = $ average industry import penetration, $size = $ log average employment, $rent = $ average rent/value-added, $FP = $ interest payments/cash flow.

The *SC* variables take the value 1 if the largest shareholder is dominant, zero otherwise. These dominant shareholder dummies are in three categories. SC_1 refers to the

Table 2.1
(continued)

largest shareholder being an insurance company, pension fund or bank. SC_2 refers to the largest shareholder being directly connected to the company either as a family member or as part of the company pension fund. SC_3 indicates that the largest shareholder is a non-financial company. $SC90$ (95) is a dummy which equals one if the probability of the leading shareholder winning a vote is 90% (95%). See Leech and Leahy 1991 or the text for more details.
(ii) All equations include fourteen industry dummies and time dummies. The remainder of table 2.2, notes (ii), (iii) also apply.

may all be considered satisficing, since ownership and management are separated. So, while these provide indirect evidence, they do not show that there is a differential impact on profit-maximizing and satisficing firms, and thus do not provide direct evidence for this theory.

One paper that does look at this question directly is by Nickell, Nicolitsas, and Dryden (1997). Taking a similar approach to that of Nickell (1996), the authors include various measures of competition and ownership structure in an augmented productivity growth equation. Specifically, in relation to testing prediction 2, they look at the impact of different share ownership structures among firms listed on the London Stock Exchange. The variable of primary interest is the concentration of ownership in a single controlling institution, which is taken to indicate fewer agency problems, since concentrated owners have a very high probability of winning a shareholder's vote.

The results of their estimation of the equivalent of equation (2.5), with additional terms for dominant shareholder and dominant shareholder interacted with rents, are shown in table 2.1.

One first notes that the results in this table corroborate Nickell 1996 in finding that firms earning higher levels of rent (i.e., facing less competition) have lower rates of TFP growth. Column 1 shows that, among London Stock Exchange–listed firms (so all firms where ownership and management are separated), those firms that have a financial institution as a dominant shareholder have significantly higher rates of TFP growth (3.2 percentage points higher). However, other types of dominant shareholders are not associated with faster growth. The term of prime interest to us here is the interaction between product market competition and the dominant shareholder dummy. If the model outlined previously is correct, then we would expect an increase in product market competition to have a greater impact on productivity growth in those firms where managers were not being effectively monitored, namely, those that did not have a dominant shareholder. This means that one would expect to see a positive coefficient on the interaction term between Nickell, Nicolitsas, and Dryden's (inverse) measure of competition and the dominant share ownership dummy. This is exactly what we see in column 3 of table 2.1.

The coefficient on rents is −0.099 (with t-statistic 2.8), on dominant financial institution shareholder is −0.011 (with t-statistic 1.1), and on the interaction is 0.39 (with t-statistic 3.3). These results suggest, first of all, that increasing competition by, for example, reducing the ratio of rents to value added from 15 percent to 5 percent increases annual TFP growth by around one percent. Once the interaction term is included, there is no direct impact of a dominant shareholder on growth. The interaction term indicates a strong degree of substitution—firms with no dominant shareholder (i.e., those that are most satisficing) will experience the full effect of competition. Those firms with a dominant shareholder do not experience higher TFP growth as a result of increased competition (in fact, they experience a decline). These results provide support for proposition 2.

However, other papers reach contradictory findings. For example, Grosfeld and Tressel (2002) consider the impact of product market competition and the concentration of ownership on productivity growth by looking at firms on the Warsaw Stock Exchange. They take a very similar approach to that of Nickell, Nicolitsas, and Dryden, but find instead that PMC and ownership concentration are complements. In addition, Grosfeld and Tressel find a nonlinear effect of competition on growth.

Grosfeld and Tressel estimate a specification of the form discussed previously and used in Nickell 1996 and in Nickell, Nicolitsas, and Dryden 1997—productivity growth is regressed on measures of competition and ownership structure. Their results of interest to us here are as follows:

1. The impact of increased PMC on firms that were previously state-owned is significant and positive. There is no effect of product market competition on new firms (created since the reforms).

2. Both more dispersed ownership and very concentrated ownership are associated with faster productivity growth, while intermediate levels of concentration are associated with the lowest rates of productivity growth.

3. Higher levels of PMC are associated with higher productivity growth in firms with either very dispersed ownership or very concen-

trated ownership. Firms with intermediate levels of ownership concentration are not significantly affected by more competition.

Overall, the evidence of a significantly stronger productivity growth impact of competition in firms that are a priori most subject to managerial slack is mixed. Our observer is thus left with doubts as to whether the popular view of competition and growth can fully account for the discrepancy between theory and empirics pointed out in chapter 1. And these doubts will only be magnified when she looks at the existing evidence on the interplay between PMC and debt pressure in light of prediction 3.

2.2.3   The Missing Complementarity Effect of Prediction 3

Prediction 3 states that debt financing and PMC are *complementary instruments* to foster productivity growth in an economy dominated by satisficing managers. This time our explorer comes back with two pieces of evidence, both of which are based on U.K. firm-level data. The first piece is again drawn from Nickell, Nicolitsas, and Dryden and their 580 U.K. manufacturing companies. The second piece is drawn from Aghion, Bloom, Blundell, Griffith, and Howitt 2003.

First consider Nickell, Nicolitsas, and Dryden's results. Table 2.2 looks at the joint impact of financial pressure and product market competition on productivity growth. Financial pressure is measured by interest payments as a share of value added, and competition is again (inversely) measured by the ratio of rent over value added. The results are similar to those found for shareholder dominance.

In column 2 of table 2.2 we see that the coefficient on financial pressure is 0.029 (with t-statistic 1.8), suggesting the greater financial pressure is associated with higher productivity growth. The coefficient of the interaction between financial pressure and rents is 0.22 (with t-statistic 2.8). This suggests that as financial pressure increases, the impact of competition decreases—that is, they are substitutes. Nickell, Nicolitsas, and Dryden illustrate the economic impact implied by these estimates—at a low level of competition (when rents are high at 25 percent of value added) the impact of increasing interest payments as a share of value added from 10 percent to 30 percent leads to an increase in productivity growth of 1.7 percentage points. At a high level of competition (when rents are 5 percent of value added), the same change in interest payments would lead to a 0.8 percentage point increase in growth. This relationship is shown in figure 2.1. This figure

Table 2.2
Impact of financial pressure and competition on productivity growth (1985–1994)

	Dependent variable: Δy_{it}	
Independent variables	1	2
Δy_{it-1}	0.03	0.05
	(0.6)	(1.1)
Δn_{it}	0.58	0.67
	(3.1)	(3.6)
Δk_{it}	0.39	0.28
$\Delta(H_{0jt}/H_{njt})$	0.78	0.73
	(3.3)	(3.1)
$10^{-3}\Delta(H_{0jt}/H_{njt}) - 1$	1.33	1.35
	(3.2)	(3.2)
$\Delta mksh_{it-2}$	−0.51	−0.50
	(2.6)	(2.6)
$conc_{j.}$	−0.020	−0.015
	(0.8)	(0.6)
$imp_{j.}$	0.25	0.23
	(1.6)	(1.5)
$10^{-2}size_i$	−0.029	0.069
	(0.2)	(0.4)
$rents_{1i}$	−0.072	−0.11
	(3.2)	(3.2)
FP_{it-1}		0.029
		(1.8)
$FP_{it-1} \times rents_{1i}$		0.22
		(2.8)
Serial correlation $[N(0,1)]$	−0.90	−0.98
Instrument validity	$\chi^2(56) = 72.3$	$\chi^2(56) = 72.0$
se	0.072	0.071
Time dummies	✓	✓
N	582	582
NT	3527	3527

Source: Nickell, Nicolitsas, and Dryden 1997, table 1.
Notes:
(i) Variables as in note (i), table 2.1.
(ii) All equations include twenty-two industry dummies and time dummies. Long-run constant returns is imposed so the coefficient on Δk is one minus the coefficients on Δy_{-1}, Δn. Δy, Δn, Δk, rents are treated as endogenous. Instruments include $y(t-2, t-3)$, $k(t-2, t-3)$, $n(t-2, t-3)$.
(iii) The equations are estimated using the Dynamic Panel Data package written by Arellano and Bond 1991 and present the robust one-step parameters that are reported in this paper to be the most reliable.

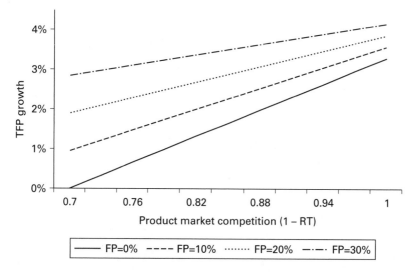

Figure 2.1
Relationship between product market competition and financial pressure and total factor productivity. Implied by Nickell, Nicolitsas, and Dryden 1997 results.

plots the values of $-0.11 * RT + 0.029 * FP + 0.22 * FP * RT$ for four values of FP (equal to zero interest payments, interest payments of 10 percent of value-added, 20 percent and 30 percent), normalized to zero at the lowest level of competition. The far right-hand end of the x-axis (where $(1 - RT) = 1$) represents perfect competition (zero rents), while the far left-hand end of the x-axis represents a low level of competition (rents of 30 percent).

Thus, financial pressure and product market competition are substitute, not complementary, engines of productivity growth. Once again, empirical work muddies the waters and leaves doubt as to whether slack reduction is really the main channel by which competition enhances growth.

The second piece of evidence relating directly to prediction 3 is from Aghion, Bloom, Blundell, Griffith, and Howitt 2003. Its authors use data on U.K. firms listed on the London Stock Exchange and look at the interaction between financial pressure (using the ratio between firms' debt and firms' cash flow) and competition (using a similar rents-based measure as Nickell (1996)). They identify the firms facing the highest financial pressure and consider whether the impact of competition differs for them relative to the whole sample of firms in a regression of the form

$$P_{it} = \exp((\beta_1 + \beta_2 F_{it})RT_{jt} + (\beta_3 + \beta_4 F_{it})RT_{jt}^2 + \beta_3 F_{it} + X'_{it}\beta_4),$$

where P is a (citation-weighted) count of firms' patenting activity, RT is rents over value added as previously, F is financial pressure (debt over cash flow), and X is a vector of other covariates. Two things to point out about the difference between this model and the ones discussed earlier are that the competition measure here is at the industry rather than the firm level (though Aghion, Bloom, Blundell, Griffith, and Howitt show that similar results are achieved with a firm-level measure) and that the explanatory variable is a direct measure of innovation, the citation-weighted patent count, rather than TFP growth.

Figure 2.2 depicts the relationship between product market competition and innovation for the whole sample of firms (the middle line with circles) and for firms facing greater financial pressure (the upper line with triangles) and lower financial pressure (the lower line with squares). First, we see that at any level of competition, firms facing a higher debt pressure innovate more. The interpretation is that innovation allows firms to escape the threat of bankruptcy. However, the

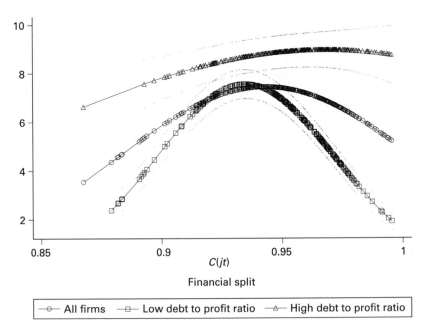

Figure 2.2
Relationship product market competition and financial pressure and patents. *Source:* Aghion, Bloom, Blundell, Griffith, and Howitt 2003, figure 16

impact of tougher financial pressure on innovation appears to be the same at all levels of competition, to the extent that the triangle line and the circle line are essentially parallel. In other words, figure 2.2 suggests that financial pressure and competition are neither complementary nor substitute engines of innovation and productivity growth.

Thus, financial pressure and competition are found to be substitutes in Nickell, Nicolitsas, and Dryden 1997 and non-interactive forces in Aghion, Bloom, Blundell, Griffith, and Howitt 2003. If slack reduction were the main channel through which competition enhanced productivity growth, then according to prediction 3 we should have found a positive interaction between the two forces.

2.3 Conclusion

Overall, our explorer does not have much to show from her investigation of the slack-reducing effects of competition on productivity growth. While competition appears to be effective at improving productivity *levels* in satisficing firms (those plagued with agency problems and managerial slack), this does not automatically translate into higher rates of productivity *growth* in such firms relative to more profit-maximizing ones. Moreover, we do not observe the complementarity between hard budget constraints and competition that should exist if the economy were truly dominated by satisficing firms and managers.

Our brave explorer is thus disheartened. She is back at stage zero in her attempt to reconcile theory and evidence on the relationship between competition and growth. She may first fall into depression, although after some thought on the matter, she may see at least two reasons for hope.

1. The approach in this chapter remained too "Schumpeterian" in the sense that a higher monetary responsiveness of managers—for example, through bonuses, stock-options, or equity holdings—will always push toward a more negative (or less positive) effect of PMC on efficiency and productivity growth. As we will argue in the next chapter, the latter prediction follows from the fact that, as in previous endogenous growth models, firms that do not innovate make zero profits; this in turn implies that PMC only affects *post-innovation* rents, not *pre-innovation* rents.

2. Not distinguishing between *pre-innovation* rents and *post-innovation* rents also has important consequences for policy design. In particular, we cannot explain the coexistence of patent policy (aimed at encouraging R&D) and antitrust (or entry-enhancing) policy aimed at fostering competition. The former appear to increase χ whereas the latter appear to reduce it. For example, if firms are profit-maximizing, patent protection (or, more generally, better protection of intellectual property rights) will enhance growth by increasing χ and therefore potential rewards from innovation. However, pro-competition policies tend to discourage innovation and growth by reducing χ and thereby forcing incumbent innovators to charge a lower limit price. And conversely, patent protection will discourage innovation by satisficing managers whereas competition policy will encourage it. In any case, why are both patent protection and antitrust policy used at the same time? Our analysis would instead suggest that we put the emphasis on patent protection if firms are (mainly) profit-maximizing, and on competition policy if firms are (mainly) non-profit-maximizing. But this seems at odds with what we observe in practice.

The next two chapters describe the successive steps leading our observer from failure to success, going from the discussion in section 1.1 to a full-fledged theory of competition and growth with incumbent innovation, which both squares the circle of reconciling theory and evidence and produces more relevant policy advice, for example, on patent protection and competition policy as complementary instruments to foster productivity growth.

3 Reconciling Theory and Evidence

In chapter 2 our explorer considered common wisdom for the observed positive correlation between product market competition and productivity growth, whereby competition should stimulate productivity growth by acting as an incentive scheme for cost reduction or quality improvements in firms run by satisficing managers. While she found convincing evidence that competition increases efficiency *levels* in firms with weak outside shareholders and/or with low debt pressure, she did not find equally strong support for a positive interaction between competition and debt pressure or competition and ownership concentration in fostering productivity *growth*.

Beyond the lack of empirical support, this explanation suffers from two additional problems. First, it does not explain the coexistence in most developed economies of patent protection legislations and R&D subsidies on the one hand, and of antitrust legislations and competition policies on the other hand. Second, it predicts a monotonic relationship between competition and the rates of innovation and productivity growth: Either the economy is dominated by profit-maximizing firms, in which case PMC should have an unambiguously negative effect on productivity growth, or the economy is dominated by large firms marred with agency problems, in which case PMC should have an unambiguously positive effect on innovation and productivity growth.

Taking stock of these limits of the common wisdom, in this chapter our explorer makes a second attempt to reconcile theory and evidence on competition and growth. This attempt also takes the endogenous growth model of chapter 1 as a benchmark, but it extends that model by allowing incumbent firms to innovate. In the extended model, innovation incentives depend not so much on post-innovation rents per se, but rather upon the difference between post-innovation and pre-innovation rents (the latter were equal to zero in the basic model where all innovations were made by outsiders).[24] In this case, more PMC may end up fostering innovations and growth because it may reduce a firm's pre-innovation rents by more than it reduces its post-innovation rents. In other words, competition may increase the incremental profits from innovating and thereby encourage R&D investments aimed at "escaping competition." Moreover, to the extent that patent policy enhances post-innovation rents, whereas competition policy reduces pre-innovation rents, having innovation incentives depend upon the difference between pre- and post-innovation rents introduces a natural reason for complementarity between the two instruments.

Our explorer first finds three key empirical predictions derived from the new extended model. The first prediction is that the relationship between product market competition and innovation is an *inverted-U shape:* that is, the escape competition effect tends to dominate for low initial levels of competition, whereas the Schumpeterian effect tends to dominate at higher levels of PMC. This prediction is in line with earlier findings of Scherer (1965a,b), Levin, Cohen, and Mowery (1985), and others.[25] The second prediction is that the average technological distance between leaders and followers across industries increases with product market competition as higher competition reduces pre-innovation rents to a larger extent in neck-and-neck sectors where firms are initially more technologically similar. In other words, it is particularly in neck-and-neck sectors where increased competition will foster innovation in order to "escape the competitor," thereby reducing the expected time interval during which an industry remains neck-and-neck. Third, the higher the average proportion of neck-and-neck industries in the economy, the stronger the "escape competition" effect on average growth and therefore the steeper the positive part of the inverted-U relationship between PMC and innovation.

When seeing these predictions confronted with data from a panel of U.K. firms, our explorer finally feels as though she has made substantial progress. The empirical results do indeed confirm the existence of an inverted-U-shaped relationship between product market competition and innovations. She also finds a similar inverted-U-shaped relationship at the industry level and sees that this relationship tends to be steeper for firms in more neck-and-neck industries. Finally, she finds that the average degree of neck-and-neckness decreases with product market competition; in other words, the technological gap between leaders and followers increases on average as a result of more intense competition.

3.1 The Escape Competition Effect

We consider a domestic economy that takes as a given the rate of innovation in the rest of the world.[26] Thus the world technology frontier is also moving at a constant rate, with productivity $\bar{A}_t$ at the end of period t satisfying

$$\bar{A}_t = \gamma \bar{A}_{t-1},$$

where $\gamma > 1$.

In each country, the final good is produced using the same kind of technology as in the previous sections, with a continuum of intermediate inputs, and we normalize the labor supply at $L = 1$, so that

$$y_t = \int_0^1 A_{it}^{1-\alpha} x_{it}^{\alpha} \, di,$$

where, in each sector i, only one firm produces intermediate input i using final good as capital according to a one-for-one technology.

In each sector, the incumbent firm faces a competitive fringe of firms that can produce the same kind of intermediate good, although at a higher unit cost. More specifically, we assume that at the end of period t, at unit cost χ, where we assume $1 < \chi < 1/\alpha < \gamma\chi$, a competitive fringe of firms can produce one unit of intermediate input i of a quality equal to $\min(A_{it}, \bar{A}_{t-1})$, where A_{it} is the productivity level achieved in sector i after innovation has had the opportunity to occur in sector i within period t.

In each period t, there are three types of sectors, which we refer to as type-j sectors, with $j \in \{0, 1\}$. A type-j sector starts up at the beginning of period t with productivity $A_{it-1} = \bar{A}_{t-1-j}$; that is, j steps behind the current frontier $\bar{A}_{t-1}$. The profit flow of an incumbent firm in any sector at the end of period t will depend upon the technological position of that firm with regard to the technological frontier at the end of the period.

Between the beginning and the end of the current period t, the incumbent firm in any sector i has the possibility of innovating with positive probability. Innovations occur step-by-step: In any sector an innovation moves productivity upward by the same factor γ. Incumbent firms can affect the probability of an innovation by investing more in R&D at the beginning of the period. Namely, by investing the quadratic R&D effort $(1/2)\gamma A_{it-1}\mu^2$ incumbent firm i in a type-0 or type-1 sector innovates with probability μ. We also assume that a type-j firm that innovates at date t generates a type-0 firm at date $t+1$, whereas if it does not innovate it generates a type-1 firm.

Now consider the R&D incentives of incumbent firms in the different types of sectors at the beginning of period t, and let μ_j denote the equilibrium R&D choice in a type-j sector.

Firms in type-1 sectors, which start one step behind the current frontier at $A_{it-1} = \bar{A}_{t-2}$ at the beginning of period t, end up with productivity $A_t = \bar{A}_{t-1}$ if they successfully innovate, and with productivity $A_t = \bar{A}_{t-2}$ otherwise. In either case, the competitive fringe can produce intermediate goods of the same quality but at cost χ instead of 1; then the equilibrium profit is equal to

$$\pi_t = A_t \delta(\chi),$$

with[27]

$$\delta(\chi) = (\chi - 1)(\chi/\alpha)^{1/(\alpha-1)}.$$

Thus the net rent from innovating for a type-1 firm is equal to

$$(\bar{A}_{t-1} - \bar{A}_{t-2})\delta(\chi),$$

and therefore a type-1 firm will choose its R&D effort to solve

$$\max_{\mu}\left\{ (\bar{A}_{t-1} - \bar{A}_{t-2})\delta(\chi)\mu - \frac{1}{2}\gamma \bar{A}_{t-2}\mu^2 \right\},$$

which yields

$$\mu_1 = \left(1 - \frac{1}{\gamma}\right)\delta(\chi).$$

In particular an increase in product market competition, measured as a reduction in the unit cost χ of the competitive fringe, will reduce the innovation incentives of a type-1 firm. This we refer to as the *Schumpeterian effect* of product market competition: Competition reduces innovation incentives and therefore productivity growth by reducing the rents from innovations of type-1 firms that start below the technological frontier. This is the dominant effect, both in IO models of product differentiation and entry and in basic endogenous growth models such as the one analyzed previously. Note that type-1 firms cannot escape the fringe by innovating: Whether they innovate or not, these firms face competitors that can produce the same quality as theirs at cost χ. As we will now see, things become different in the case of type-0 firms.

Firms in type-0 sectors that start at the current frontier end up with productivity $\bar{A}_t$ if they innovate, and stay with their initial productivity $\bar{A}_{t-1}$ if they do not. But the competitive fringe can never get beyond producing quality $\bar{A}_{t-1}$. Thus, by innovating, a type-0 incumbent firm produces an intermediate good that is γ times better than the competing good the fringe could produce, and at unit cost 1 instead of χ for the fringe. Our assumption $1/\alpha < \gamma\chi$ then implies that competition by the fringe is no longer a binding constraint for an innovating incumbent, so that its equilibrium profit post-innovation will simply be the profit of an unconstrained monopolist, namely,

$$\pi_t = \bar{A}_t \delta(1/\alpha).$$

On the other hand, a type-0 firm that does not innovate will keep its productivity equal to $\bar{A}_{t-1}$. Since the competitive fringe can produce up to this quality level at cost χ, the equilibrium profit of a type-0 firm that does not innovate is equal to

$$\pi_t = \bar{A}_{t-1} \delta(\chi).$$

A type-0 firm will then choose its R&D effort to

$$\max_{\mu} \left\{ [\bar{A}_t \delta(1/\alpha) - \bar{A}_{t-1}\delta(\chi)]\mu - \frac{1}{2}\gamma\bar{A}_{t-1}\mu^2 \right\},$$

so that in equilibrium

$$\mu_0 = \delta(1/\alpha) - \frac{1}{\gamma}\delta(\chi).$$

In particular an increase in product market competition, namely, a reduction in χ, will now have a fostering effect on R&D and innovation. This, we refer to as the *escape competition effect*: competition reduces pre-innovation rents of type-0 incumbent firms, but not their post-innovation rents since by innovating these firms have escaped the fringe. This, in turn induces those firms to innovate in order to escape competition with the fringe.[28]

3.1.1 Composition Effect and the Inverted-U Relationship between Competition and Innovation

We have just seen that PMC tends to have opposite effects on frontier and lagging sectors, fostering innovation by the former and discouraging innovation by the latter. In this section we consider the impact of competition on the steady-state aggregate innovation intensity

$$I = q_0\mu_0 + q_1\mu_1, \tag{3.1}$$

where q_j is the steady-state fraction of type-j sectors (recall that type-2 sectors do not perform R&D).

To get a nontrivial steady-state fraction of type-0 firms, we need the net flows out of state 0 (which corresponds to type-0 firms that fail to innovate in the current period) to be compensated by a net flow into state 0. We have the following flow equations describing the net flows into and out of states 0 and 1:

$$q_0(1 - \mu_0) = q_1\mu_1;$$

$$q_1\mu_1 = q_0(1 - \mu_0);$$

in which the left-hand sides represent the steady-state expected flow of sectors that move out of the corresponding state j and the right-hand sides capture the net flows into state j, for $j = 2, 1$, and 0. This, together with the identity

$$q_0 + q_1 = 1,$$

implies that

$$q_0 = \frac{\mu_1}{1 + \mu_1 - \mu_0},$$

and therefore:

$$I = \mu_0\mu_1 \left[\frac{1}{1 + \mu_1 - \mu_0} + \frac{1}{1 + \mu_0 - \mu_1} \right].$$

In particular, one can see that the overall effect of increased product market competition on I is ambiguous since it produces opposite effects on innovation probabilities in type-0 and type-1 sectors (i.e., on

μ_0 and μ_1). In fact, one can say more than that and show that (1) the Schumpeterian effect always dominates for γ sufficiently large; (2) the escape competition effect always dominates for γ sufficiently close to one; (3) for intermediate values of γ, the escape competition effect dominates when competition is initially low (with χ close to $1/\alpha$) whereas the Schumpeterian effect dominates when competition is initially high (with χ close to one). In this latter case, the relationship between competition and innovation is inverted-U-shaped.

This inverted-U pattern can be explained as follows: At low initial levels of competition (i.e., high initial levels of $\delta(\chi)$), type-1 firms have strong reason to innovate; it follows that many intermediate sectors in the economy will end up being type-0 firms in steady state (this we refer to as the *composition effect* of competition on the relative equilibrium fractions of type-0 and type-1); but then the dominant effect of competition on innovation is the escape competition effect whereby more competition fosters innovation by type-0 firms. On the other hand, at high initial levels of competition, innovation incentives in type-1 sectors are so low that a sector will remain type-1 for a long time, and therefore many sectors will end up being type-1 in steady state, which in turn implies that the negative Schumpeterian appropriability effect of competition on innovation should tend to dominate in that case.

3.1.2 Empirical Predictions

The preceding analysis generates several interesting predictions:

1. Innovation in sectors in which firms are close to the technology frontier react positively to an increase in product market competition.

2. Innovation reacts less positively, or negatively, in sectors in which firms are further below the technological frontier.

3. The average fraction of frontier sectors decreases—namely, the average technological gap between incumbent firms and the frontier in their respective sectors increases—when competition increases.

4. The overall effect of competition on aggregate innovation is inverted-U-shaped.

These predictions have been confronted by Aghion, Bloom, Blundell, Griffith, and Howitt (2003) with U.K. firm-level data on competition and patenting, and we briefly summarize their findings in section 3.2.

3.2   Empirical Evidence

Aghion, Bloom, Blundell, Griffith, and Howitt (2003) confront these
predictions with data on the patenting activity of a panel of U.K.
firms.[29] The theoretical discussion provides a specification for the average arrival rate of innovations in an industry according to the level of
product market competition and the degree of neck-and-neckness. The
empirical specification is based on a model of the hazard rate of patenting and uses this to derive a generalized Poisson model for the citation-
weighted count of patents.

The main focus in Aghion, Bloom, Blundell, Griffith, and Howitt
2003 is to find out whether there is indeed a nonmonotonic relationship between innovation and product market competition. Therefore a
semi-parametric approach is adopted instead of the linear regressions
used in previous empirical studies. The use of semi-parametric estimators that do not impose symmetry is important because it allows
the authors to recover the possibly nonlinear relationship between
product market competition and innovation while controlling for other
covariates. The earlier literature using U.K. company data established
that indicators of the level of competition, both at the firm and the
industry level, had significant and largely positive impacts on innovation intensity at the firm level. Aghion, Bloom, Blundell, Griffith,
and Howitt extend this literature by assessing the predictions given
previously.

One of the difficulties Aghion, Bloom, Blundell, Griffith, and Howitt
face is identifying a potentially nonlinear relationship while controlling
for potential endogeneity. They take a control function approach[30] and
find a strong inverted-U relationship. The main equation of interest is a
Poisson count model of the form

$$E[P_{it} \mid c_{jt}, x_{jt}] = e^{\{g(c_{jt}) + x'_{jt}\beta\}},\tag{3.2}$$

where P is a citation-weighted patent count, c is a measure of competition in the firm's product market (measured as $1 -$ Lerner Index), and
x is a vector of other covariates. Prediction 1 suggests that $g(c_{jt})$ is nonmonotonic, and it is therefore essential to estimate equation (3.2) using
a suitably flexible functional form. The authors use a quadratic spline
with eight evenly spaced knot points to approximate $g(.)$. To control
for potential endogeneity, they specify a reduced form where competition changes as a function of number of regulatory reforms including

the EU Single Market Programme, large-scale privatizations, and anti-trust actions.

3.2.1 Data

Aghion, Bloom, Blundell, Griffith, and Howitt (2003) use two main data sources—firm-level accounting data and administrative data from the U.S. Patent Office. The accounting data come from Data-Stream and include 461 firms listed on the London Stock Exchange. The patenting information on each firm is from the U.S. Patent Office, where 236 of the firms have at least one patent. The data run from 1968 to 1997.

Innovation   Innovative output is measured using citation-weighted patents. There is a large literature on measuring innovation intensity, as discussed in chapter 1. One concern that is often expressed over using patent counts is that patents may not be comparable across firms or industries because their value can vary significantly. Therefore, the number of times a patent has been cited in other patents is used to weight the patent. This provides a measure that is more indicative of the value of the patent.

Product Market Competition   The main measure of PMC used is a measure of rents, or the Lerner Index, as used in Nickell 1996. This can also be directly derived as the appropriate measure from the preceding theory (see Aghion, Bloom, Blundell, Griffith, and Howitt 2003). Information reported in DataStream is used to construct an industry-level measure similar to Nickell's (1996) measure of rents over value-added. The Lerner Index is price minus marginal cost over price. At the firm level the Lerner Index varies from 0 to 0.38, has a mean of 0.09, and has a median value of 0.08.

One of Aghion, Bloom, Blundell, Griffith, and Howitt's major concerns is with the potential endogeneity of the competition measure—high rents spur firms to innovate, but innovation also leads to high rents. Industry effects remove the bias that results from correlation between permanent levels of innovative activity and PMC. The authors also instrument PMC with a large number of policy reforms. The United Kingdom over this period provides an extremely rich environment within which to study the impact of PMC on innovation behavior. Not only is there a long panel of detailed company data, but this period also saw a number of significant, and largely exogenous, changes in PMC. These changes, which altered the structure of product markets across industries, included the implementation of the European Single Market Program, a series of structural and behavioral reforms imposed on different industries as a result of investigations by the Monopolies and Mergers Commission (MMC) under the Fair Trading Act and large-scale privatizations.

Technology Gap or Neck-and-Neckness The size of the technology gap or the degree of neck-and-neckness within each industry is captured with a measure of the dispersion of firm-level technology and cost indicators. This is measured by the proportional distance a firm is from the technological frontier (measured by TFP). This proportional distance, m_{it}, is calculated for each firm, and the industry average

$$m_{jt}^{tfp} = \frac{1}{N_{jt}} \sum_{i \in j} m_{it}$$

is used, where N_{jt} is the number firms in industry j at time t. A lower value of m_j indicates that firms in industry j are technologically closer to the frontier (and therefore more like the neck-and-neck firms), while a high value of m_j indicates a large technological gap.

3.2.2   Empirical Results

Figure 3.1 shows a strong inverted-U relationship between innovation, as measured by the citation-weighted patent count, and product market competition. The uneven curve is a quadratic spline, while the smoother curve uses a straight quadratic form (i.e., $g(c_{jt}) = \beta_2 c_{jt} + \beta_2 c_{jt}^2$). The dotted lines are 95 percent confidence bands on the quadratic. The exponential quadratic specification provides a very reasonable approximation and retains the clear inverted U. The underlying distribution of the data is shown by the intensity of the points on the estimated curves. These indicate that the peak of the inverted U lies near the median of the distribution (the median is 0.95). A simple linear relationship would yield a positive slope, which confirms the results discussed in chapter 2 and shown in figure 1.3. Aghion, Bloom, Blundell, Griffith, and Howitt note that controlling for endogeneity and including time and industry effects shift the peak toward the competitive direction but still suggest the importance of the Schumpeterian effect for a significant minority of firms and industries.

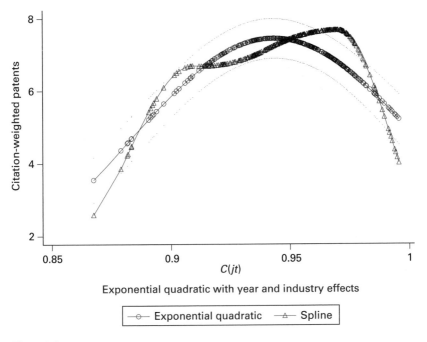

Figure 3.1
Innovation and product market competition: Exponential quadratic and the semipara-
metric specifications, with year and industry effects. *Source:* Aghion, Bloom, Blundell,
Griffith, and Howitt 2003, figure 8

Aghion, Bloom, Blundell, Griffith, and Howitt also show that the
inverted-U relationship holds within several industries. Figure 3.2
presents the relationship fitted separately for each of the top four innovating industries—motor vehicles; chemicals; electrical and electronic;
and food, beverages, and tobacco. In each case there is an inverted-U
shape.

The second prediction is that this effect will be stronger in industries that are less neck-and-neck—that is, in industries in which
firms' technology is more dispersed. The authors look at the importance of similarities in technology across firms in the same industry—
defined by the size of the technology gap or the degree of neck-and-
neckness. The theory predicts that the inverted-U-shaped relationship between competition and growth should be steeper for more
neck-and-neck industries. Figure 3.3 shows that a subsample of
their data—industries with below-median technological gap (so more

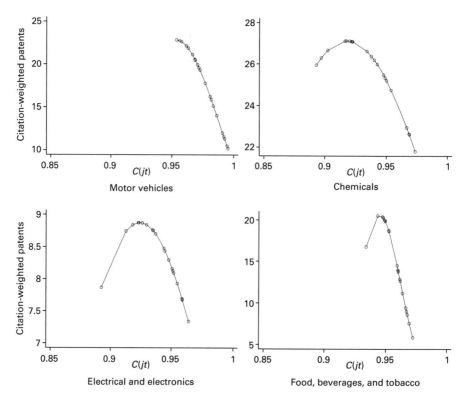

Figure 3.2
Innovation and product market competition: Four highest patenting industries. *Source:*
Aghion, Bloom, Blundell, Griffith, and Howitt 2003, figure 10

neck-and-neck industries)—have a higher level of innovation activity
for any level of product market competition and that the inverted-U
curve is steeper.

The third key prediction, derived from the theoretical discussion, is
that in equilibrium the average technology gap between leaders and
followers should be an increasing function of the overall level of indus-
trywide competition (so that average neck-and-neckness should be a
decreasing function of competition). Figure 3.4 presents a kernel-
smoothed plot of average technological distance from the frontier for
each industry time observation against the industry competition index.
This shows a strongly positive relationship, as predicted by the theory.
In particular, more competitive industries display a lower degree of
neck-and-neckness.

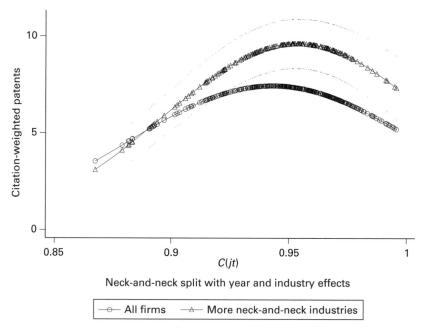

Figure 3.3
Innovation and product market competition: The neck-and-neck split. *Source:* Aghion,
Bloom, Blundell, Griffith, and Howitt 2003, figure 15

3.3 Conclusion

Our explorer has seen that going back to the inspirational source of
theoretical IO has allowed us to extend the endogenous growth model
of chapter 1 so as to allow for incumbent innovation and for the
distinction between neck-and-neck and lagging sectors. This enriched
model delivered three main predictions, all of which appeared to
be vindicated by U.K. firm-level data on competition as measured
by rents and innovation as measured by patenting. First, increasing
PMC has a positive effect on innovation starting from a low initial level
of competition, but it has a negative effect on innovation if one starts
from an already high degree of competition. Interestingly, Scherer
(1965a,b) had already hinted at such an inverted-U relationship between competition and innovation. But his remark was made en pas-
sant, on the basis of a quadratic regression but without any clear
explanation for the negative quadratic coefficient. But now our explorer knows that the inverted-U pattern has to do with the fact that

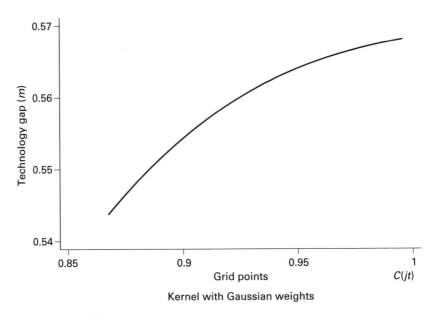

Figure 3.4
Technology gap and competition: The composition effect. *Notes:* Kernel regression, $bw = 0.05, k = 6$. *Source:* Aghion, Bloom, Blundell, Griffith, and Howitt 2003, figure 14

neck-and-neck sectors respond more positively to an increase in competition than laggard incumbents; that the closer domestic producers in an industry are to the frontier (i.e., the more "neck-and-neck" the industry is), the more positive is the effect of PMC on innovation; and that the average gap between U.K. incumbents and their frontier industries increases with product market competition.

These predictions have important policy implications for the design of competition policy. There may be ranges of competition over which it is important to weigh potential dynamic efficiency losses against static efficiency gains from tough antitrust policy, although these are not nearly as large as theory predicts. It is important to understand the impact that market liberalization and tough antitrust policy may have on laggard industries. This is not to say that these industries should be protected but that governments may want complementary institutions to cope with displacement of workers. In addition, the results suggest that competition and antitrust policy should be particularly emphasized in sectors that are currently neck-and-neck. In sectors where the domestic innovator lags behind the frontier, policy may want to facilitate innovations aimed at catching up with the frontier. This in turn will increase the equilibrium fraction of neck-and-neck sectors and thereby foster aggregate innovation since these sectors are the most innovative. Third, patent policy is a necessary complement to competition policy: The former ensures that an innovative firm is properly rewarded, whereas the latter makes it more painful *not* to innovate. However, it is important to make sure that patent legislations do not make it too hard for laggard firms to catch up with current leaders; otherwise, the economy would end up with too few neck-and-neck sectors.

Our intrepid explorer may realize that there is an important dimension of competition policy that our analysis in this chapter did not address—namely, entry regulation (or deregulation). A recent report entitled *An Agenda for a Growing Europe* (Sapir 2004), produced for the European Commission, points out that the practice of competition policy in the European Union may put too much emphasis on incumbent firms (making sure that no incumbent firm acquires a "dominant position") at the expense of entry considerations. However, promoting entry is as important for innovation and productivity growth as preventing collusion or predatory behavior among incumbent firms. In the next chapter, our explorer will devote her attention to the study of how increased entry affects innovation and growth across different types of sectors of the domestic economy.

4 The Escape Entry Effect

This chapter focuses on the effect of (foreign) entry on innovation and productivity growth in incumbent firms. In particular, we are interested in the extent to which the effect of liberalizing entry on innovation and productivity growth depends upon the technological distance between the domestic incumbent and the world technology frontier.

Our main findings will be, first, that reducing barriers to entry to foreign products and firms has an overall positive effect on innovation and productivity growth. Second, it has a more positive effect on economic performance for firms and industries that are initially closer to the technological frontier. In contrast, performance in firms and industries that are initially far from the frontier may actually be damaged by liberalization. As a result, liberalization magnifies the initial differences in productivity. This is because incumbent firms that are sufficiently close to the technological frontier can survive and deter entry by innovating. An increased entry threat thus results in higher innovation intensity aimed at escaping that threat. In contrast, firms and sectors that are far below the frontier are in a weaker position to fight external entry. For these firms, an increase in the entry threat reduces the expected payoff from innovating, since their expected life horizon has become shorter.

A third finding is that the institutional environment in which firms function has a central bearing on whether or not they benefit from liberalization. Here, our focus is on labor market institutions, which affect the distribution of rents between firms and workers. More precisely, our theory predicts that the response of innovative investments to liberalization is dampened in regions with more pro-worker labor regulations. Thus, in relative terms, trade reforms hurt growth in regions with pro-labor regulations, while enhancing growth in regions with pro-employer regulations.

The chapter is organized as follows. Section 4.2 sketches a theoretical framework that links liberalization and entry to industrial performance across heterogeneous industries and summarizes its main implications. Section 4.3 shows the impact of increased foreign entry on productivity growth and patenting using a U.K. firm-level panel data set for the period 1987–1993. Section 4.4 reports similar results by Aghion, Burgess, Redding, and Zilibotti (2003) on the impact of the Indian liberalization experiment of 1991 using a three-digit state-industry panel for the period 1980–1997, and also the findings from a cross-country analysis of the impact of deregulation across OECD countries by Nicoletti and Scarpetta (2003). Section 4.5 concludes.

4.1   A Simple Growth Model with Entry

4.1.1   The Framework
The following framework, developed in parallel work by Aghion, Burgess, Redding, and Zilibotti (2003) and Aghion, Blundell, Griffith, Howitt, and Prantl (2003) is again a straight extension of the model in chapter 1. It enriches the model in the previous chapter by introducing potential entry in each intermediate sector, then focusing on the effects of entry threat on incumbents' innovative investments and thereby on productivity growth, both at the level of different industries and on average in the overall economy. Instead, the previous chapter was concerned with the growth effects of increased competition among incumbent firms.

All agents live for one period. In each period t a final good (henceforth the numeraire) is produced by a competitive sector using a continuum one of intermediate inputs, according to the technology

$$y_t = \int_0^1 A_t(i)^{1-\alpha} x_t(i)^\alpha \, dv],$$

where $x_t(i)$ is the quantity of intermediate input produced in sector i at date t, $A_t(i)$ is a productivity parameter that measures the quality of the intermediate input i in producing the final good, and $\alpha \in (0, 1)$. The final good can be used either for consumption, or as an input in the process of production of intermediate goods, or for investments in innovation.

In each intermediate sector i only one firm (a monopolist) is active in each period. Thus the variable i refers both to an intermediate sector (industry) and to the intermediate firm that is active in that sector.

Like any other agent in the economy, intermediate producers live for one period only and property rights over intermediate firms are transmitted within dynasties. Intermediate firms use labor and capital (the final good) as inputs. As shown in chapter 1, the equilibrium profit for each intermediate firm will take the form

$$\pi_t(i) = \delta A_t(i), \tag{4.1}$$

where δ may reflect either the degree of product market competition, as in the previous chapters, or the bargaining power of the firm vis-à-vis its workers, with a higher δ corresponding to a more pro-employer labor market environment.

4.1.2   Technology and Entry

Let $\bar{A}_t$ denote the new frontier productivity at date t and assume that

$$\bar{A}_t = \gamma \bar{A}_{t-1}$$

with $\gamma = 1 + g > 1$. We will emphasize the distinction, made in the previous chapter, between sectors in which the incumbent producer is "neck-and-neck" with the frontier and those in which the incumbent firm is far below the frontier.

At date t an intermediate firm can either be close to the frontier, with productivity level $A_{t-1}(i) = \bar{A}_{t-1}$ (type-1 sector i), far below the frontier, with productivity level $A_{t-1}(i) = \bar{A}_{t-2}$ (type-2 sector i), or very far below the frontier, with productivity level $A_{t-1}(i) = \bar{A}_{t-3}$ (type-3 sector i).

Before they produce and generate profits, firms can innovate to increase their productivity. Each innovation increases the firm's productivity by the factor γ. For innovation to be successful with probability z, a type-j intermediate firm with $j \in \{1, 2\}$ at date t must invest

$$c_{tj}(z) = \frac{1}{2} c z^2 A_{t-j}(i).$$

However, as a result of knowledge spillovers, type-3 firms are automatically upgraded by one step, so they do not need to invest in innovation.

Intermediate firms are subject to an entry threat from foreign producers. Let p denote the probability that an entrant shows up. Liberalization corresponds to an increase in p. Foreign entrants at date t are assumed to operate with the end-of-period frontier productivity, $\bar{A}_t$. This is in line with the large literature on the multinational firm and the OLI framework (see Caves 1974).

If the foreign firm enters and competes with a local firm, which has a lower productivity, it takes over the market and becomes the new incumbent firm in the sector. If it competes with a local firm that has the same productivity, however, Bertrand competition drives the profits of both the local and the foreign firm to zero. Now, suppose that potential entrants observe the post-innovation technology of the incumbent firm before deciding whether or not to enter. Then the foreign firm will find it profitable to enter only if the local firm has a post-innovation productivity level lower than the frontier. However, the foreign firm will never enter in period t if the local firm has achieved the frontier productivity level $\bar{A}_t$. Therefore, the probability of actual entry in any intermediate sector i is equal to zero when the local firm v is initially close to the frontier and has successfully innovated, and it is equal to p otherwise.

4.1.3 Equilibrium Innovation Investments
Using equation (4.1), together with the previous innovation technology, we can analyze the innovation decisions by intermediate firms that are close to and far below the frontier. Firms that are initially far below the frontier at date t choose their investment so as to maximize expected profits net of R&D costs, namely,

$$\max_z \left\{ \delta[z(1-p)\bar{A}_{t-1} + (1-z)(1-p)\bar{A}_{t-2}] - \frac{1}{2}cz^2\bar{A}_{t-2} \right\},$$

so that by the first-order condition the level of R&D in type-2 sectors is

$$z_2 = \frac{\delta}{c}(1-p)(\gamma - 1). \tag{4.2}$$

Firms that are initially close to the frontier choose their investment so as to

$$\max_z \left\{ \delta[z\bar{A}_t + (1-z)(1-p)\bar{A}_{t-1}] - \frac{1}{2}cz^2\bar{A}_{t-1} \right\}$$

so that the level of R&D in type-1 sectors is

$$z_1 = \frac{\delta}{c}(\gamma - 1 + p). \tag{4.3}$$

We interpret an increase in the threat of product entry, p, as a liberalization reform. Straightforward differentiation of equilibrium innovation intensities with respect to p yields

$$\frac{\partial z_1}{\partial p} = \delta/c > 0;$$

$$\frac{\partial z_2}{\partial p} = -\delta(\gamma - 1)/c < 0.$$

In other words, *increasing the threat of entry encourages innovation in advanced firms and discourages it in backward firms*. The intuition for these comparative statics is immediate. The higher the threat of entry, the more instrumental innovations will be in helping incumbent firms already close to the technological frontier retain the local market. However, firms that are already far behind the frontier have no chance of winning against a potential entrant. Thus, in that case, a higher threat of entry will only lower the expected net gain from innovation, thereby reducing ex ante incentives to invest in innovation.

Next, consider the effects of changes in labor market regulations on innovative investments:

$$\frac{\partial z_1}{\partial \delta} = \frac{1}{c}(\gamma - 1 + p) > 0;$$

$$\frac{\partial z_2}{\partial \delta} = \frac{1}{c}(1 - p)g > 0.$$

We find that *pro-employer labor market regulations encourage innovation in all firms*. If we look at the cross-partial derivatives with respect to entry threat (p) and labor regulation (δ), we get

$$\frac{\partial^2 z_1}{\partial \delta \partial p} = \frac{1}{c} > 0;$$

$$\frac{\partial^2 z_2}{\partial \delta \partial p} = -(\gamma - 1)/c < 0.$$

Thus, in particular, *a more pro-employer labor regulation*, namely, a higher δ, *increases the positive impact of entry on innovation investments in type-1 industries*, though not in type-2 sectors.

Finally, we can derive the steady-state fractions of type-j sectors, q_j, using the steady-state flow equations

$$p(1 - q_1) = (1 - p)(1 - z_1)q_1, \tag{4.4}$$

$$(1 - p)(1 - z_1)q_1 = pq_2 + (1 - p)(1 - z_2)q_2,$$

where

$q_1 + q_2 + q_3 = 1$.

The left-hand sides of equation (4.4) refer to the net flows of sectors into type-1 and type-2, whereas the right-hand sides refer to the net flows out of type-1 and type-2.

In Aghion, Blundell, Griffith, Howitt, and Prantl 2003 we show that the average rate of productivity growth among incumbent firms

$$G = (\gamma - 1)(q_1 z_1 + q_2 z_2 + q_3)$$

is increasing in p when δ/c is small, and therefore when the R&D cost c is sufficiently high.

4.1.4   Main Theoretical Predictions

We conclude this section by summarizing our main findings in Aghion, Blundell, Griffith, Howitt, and Prantl 2003:

1. Liberalization (as measured by an increase in the threat of entry) encourages innovation in industries that are initially close to the frontier and discourages innovation in industries that are far from it.

2. When the R&D cost is sufficiently large, liberalization increases average productivity growth among incumbent firms.

3. Pro-worker labor market regulations discourage innovation and growth in all industries, and the negative effect increases with liberalization.

In the following section we report on three recent papers that confront these predictions with firm- or industry-level data. Aghion, Blundell, Griffith, Howitt, and Prantl 2003 provides empirical evidence for the first two predictions based on U.K. firm-level panel data. Aghion, Burgess, Redding, and Zilibotti (2003) test the third prediction using industry-level data from India. Nicoletti and Scarpatta 2003 looks at industries across OECD countries.

4.2   Entry and Growth in the United Kingdom

4.2.1   Estimated Equations and Measures

Aghion, Blundell, Griffith, Howitt, and Prantl (2003) look at the effect of entry on performance and productivity growth in the United Kingdom. As discussed in chapter 1, the United Kingdom is a good place to study these issues because there have been substantial policy reforms that liberalized product and factor markets and opened up the

United Kingdom to foreign direct investment. In addition, the United Kingdom has industries that are both close to and far from the technological frontier, and there is availability of rich micro data on productivity growth, patenting activity, and actual entry.

Following the theory outlined previously, Aghion, Blundell, Griffith, Howitt, and Prantl look at the relationship between foreign firm entry and growth in total factor productivity, and how this relationship varies with the industries' distance to the technological frontier. The main equation of interest is of the form

$$Y_{ijt} = f(E_{jt}, F_{jt}, X_{ijt}),$$ (4.5)

where i indexes (incumbent) firms, j indexes industries (four-digit), and t indexes years. Y is a measure of incumbent firm growth in TFP or innovative performance, E is the actual entry rate of foreign firms, F is the industries' distance to the technological frontier, and X is a vector of other firm and/or industry covariates that control for other economic processes that may affect the innovative performance of domestic incumbent firms.

One of the main concerns in estimating this relationship is the likelihood that entry is endogenous—entry is more attractive in industries where expectuations about future productivity growth are high. To control for unobservable industry characteristics and common macro shocks, Aghion, Blundell, Griffith, Howitt, and Prantl include dummies. However, these may not be sufficient to remove all spurious correlation between entry and the growth in TFP (or patent count). In particular, relative changes in the entry rate across industries may be indirectly caused by shocks to U.K. TFP growth (or patenting). The approach taken to remove this temporal correlation is to use policy and foreign technology variables as excluded instruments that determine entry but have no direct effect on the growth in TFP (or patenting). The instruments used are investigations and decisions by the Monopoly and Merger Commission, privatization cases of large publicly owned companies, and indicators for three-digit industries expected to be highly affected by the EU Single Market Programme. Thus Aghion, Blundell, Griffith, Howitt, and Prantl specify the following reduced form equation for entry:

$$E_{jt} = Z'_{jt}\Pi + F_{jt}\psi + X_{ijt}\phi + v_{jt},$$ (4.6)

with

$$E[v_{jt} \mid Z_{jt}, F_{jt}, X_{ijt}] = 0 \tag{4.7}$$

where Z_{it} denote the instruments.

Innovative performance is measured in two ways. First, growth in TFP is measured using data on output and factor inputs at the plant level for the population of U.K. manufacturing enterprises. Second, patent counts are used. These are available for a subset of firms (those listed on the U.K. Stock Market). Entry is measured either by the actual number of employees in new foreign plants or by entry rates into four-digit industries in the previous periods. Distance to frontier is measured by relative labor productivity between U.K. and U.S. industry at the four-digit level.

4.2.2 Data

The empirical models specified previously are estimated using micro-level data on productivity growth and patenting activity of British firms between 1987 and 1993. Data is combined from three main sources. First, data from the Annual Respondents Database (ARD) is used. This covers the manufacturing sector and contains the micro data underlying the Annual Census of Production. It is collected by the British Office for National Statistics under the 1947 Statistical Trade Act, and response is mandatory. Second, data from the IFS Leverhulme database that links patent data from the NBER/Case Western Patent database with firm-level accounting data from DataStream is used. The patent database contains all patents granted by the U.S. Patent Office between 1968 and 1999. This patent data is linked to DataStream data on 415 firms listed on the London Stock Exchange during the time period 1968–1996. Third, data from the NBER Productivity Database is used to measure distance to frontier.[31]

4.2.3 The Aggregate Effect of Entry

The impact of entry on growth in TFP is positive and significant, as shown in table 4.1. The first two columns of the table show the results using an OLS estimator. As discussed previously, one of the main concerns addressed in Aghion, Blundell, Griffith, Howitt, and Prantl 2003 is that entry is endogenous, and therefore in columns (3) and (4) they instrument entry using a large number of policy variables. The coefficient gets larger when an IV estimator is used and the control function is significant, which indicates a negative endogeneity bias. In addition, the Sargan test indicates no rejection of the over-identifying restrictions.

Table 4.1
The effect of foreign entry on total factor productivity growth of domestic incumbents

Independent variables	Dependent variable: growth of total factor productivity$_{ijt}$			
	OLS	OLS	IV	IV
Change(foreign plant employment)$_{jt}$	0.0857**	0.0840*	0.3814***	0.3823**
	(0.0397)	(0.0430)	(0.1444)	(0.1752)
year indicators	Yes	Yes	Yes	Yes
4-digit industry indicators	Yes		Yes	
establishment fixed effects		Yes		Yes
Test results				
exogeneity of change(foreign plant employment)$_{jt}$, *t*-statistic			−2.12**	−1.72*
over-identifying restrictions, χ^2-statistic (# restrictions)			29.42(30)	32.40(30)
significance of policy indicators and US R&D intensity in first stage regression, *F*-statistic			4.71(31)***	18.71(31)***
#(observations)	32,339	32,339	32,339	32,339

Source: Aghion, Blundell, Griffith, Howitt, and Prantl 2003, table 1. Authors' calculations using ONS data and other data sources. All statistical results remain Crown Copyright. *Notes:* OLS regression results with robust standard errors in brackets are displayed. Standard errors are clustered on the four-digit industry level. Observations are weighted by the inverse of their sampling weight times their employment. The sample consists of 32,339 observations on 3,827 domestic incumbent establishments between 1981 and 1993. *** (**, *) indicate significance at the 1- (5-, 10-) percent significance level.

The estimated impact of entry on TFP growth is also economically significant. Increasing the entry rate from the mean by one standard deviation (from 0.44% to 3.8%) would result in a rise in the average growth rate of TFP of about 1.3 percentage points.

4.2.4 The Escape Entry and Discouragement Effects

An important feature missing from this analysis is the fact that the impact of entry may vary across industries, and in particular it is likely to vary with the state of technology of the industry. In a second paper, Aghion, Blundell, Griffith, Howitt, and Prantl (2004) interact entry with the incumbent's distance to the technology frontier. Their results suggest that there is a significant effect of the foreign entry rate on productivity growth and that this varies with distance to the frontier, as shown in table 4.2. The interaction between entry and distance to

Table 4.2
Total factor productivity growth models

Independent variables	Dependent variable: Growth of total factor productivity$_{i,t}$		
	(1)	(2)	(3-IV of 1)
Entry$_{j,t-1}$*Distance to frontier$_{j,t-1 \text{ to } t-3}$	−3.338***		−3.128***
	(1.103)		(1.325)
Foreign firm entry rate$_{j,t-1}$	1.384***		2.575***
	(0.398)		(0.435)
Entry$_{j,t-1}$*D(high distance$_{j,t-1 \text{ to } t-3}$)		1.192***	
		(0.285)	
Entry$_{j,t-1}$*D(med. distance$_{j,t-1 \text{ to } t-3}$)		0.525*	
		(0.310)	
Entry$_{j,t-1}$*D(low distance$_{j,t-1 \text{ to } t-3}$)		−0.786*	
		(0.450)	
Distance to frontier$_{j,t-1 \text{ to } t-3}$	0.062**	0.059**	0.061**
	(0.027)	(0.026)	(0.026)
Lerner index$_{j,t-1}$	−0.155***	−0.154***	−0.151***
	(0.055)	(0.054)	(0.054)
Market share$_{i,t-1}$	−1.191***	−1.189***	−1.186***
	(0.305)	(0.305)	(0.298)
R^2, red. Form, entry			0.2338
F, instruments			3.08 (7)***
t, exogeneity, entry			−3.44***
R^2, red. Form, interaction			0.2263
F, instruments			2.18 (7)**
t, exogeneity, interaction			0.59
χ^2, over identification			8.80 (6)
Year dummies	Yes	Yes	Yes
Establishment fixed effects	Yes	Yes	Yes
#(observations)	26,607	26,607	26,607

Source: Aghion, Blundell, Griffith, Howitt, and Prantl 2004, table 1. Authors' calculations using ONS data and other data sources. All statistical results remain Crown Copyright. *Notes:* OLS and 2SLS regression results with robust standard errors in brackets. Clustering on the industry level and sampling probability weights taken into account. In column (3) displaying 2SLS results standard errors are not corrected for two-stage procedure. The sample consists of 26,607 observations on domestic incumbent establishments between 1987 and 1993. *** (**, *) indicates significance at the 1- (5-, 10-) percent significance level.

frontier suggests that the effect of entry on TFP growth is all the more positive when an industry is closer to the technological frontier.

This result is robust to instrumentation, as shown in column (3). Aghion, Blundell, Griffith, Howitt, and Prantl (2004) also show that this result holds up to using an alternative measure of innovation and growth, a count of patent applications made by firms.

4.3   The Indian Liberalization Experiment

Another empirical paper that directly tests the predictions of this theory is Aghion, Burgess, Redding, and Zilibotti 2003. It authors look at industry-level data for Indian states and compare performance before and after a large-scale reform that liberalized entry. In India, up to the mid-eighties, the central government maintained control over industrial development through public ownership, licensing and high tariff and non-tariff barriers, and controls on foreign investment. The New Industrial Policy, introduced in 1991, involved trade liberalization (there was a 51 percent reduction in tariffs with 97 percent of products experiencing tariff reductions, and quantitative controls on imports of intermediate products were also largely eliminated), the approval of foreign technology agreements and foreign investents with up to 51 percent of equity made automatic in a large number of industries, and deregulation (the requirements to obtain a license to start up a new production unit, expand production levels by more than 25 percent, or to manufacture a new product were removed in the majority of industrial sectors; the number of industrial sectors reserved for the public sector was also dramatically reduced). Aghion, Burgess, Redding, and Zilibotti use data at a three-digit state-industry level and look across pre- and post-reform periods, examining whether being closer to the Indian technological frontier or having more pro-employer labor institutions pre-reform affects post-reform performance. They run regressions of the form

$$y_{ist} = \alpha_{is} + \beta_t + \gamma_i t + \delta(x_{is})(d_t) + \eta r_{st} + \theta(r_s)(d_t) + u_{ist}, \tag{4.8}$$

where i indexes three-digit industries, s indexes the Indian state in which the industry is located, and t indexes years; y_{ist} is a three-digit state-industry manufacturing performance outcome expressed in logs; and x_{is} is pre-reform distance to the Indian technological frontier defined as labor productivity in a three-digit state-industry in 1990 divided by labor productivity in the most productive three-digit state-industry in that year. This measure equals 1 for the frontier and is less than 1 for non-frontier state-industries. A higher x_{is} therefore corresponds to being closer to the technological frontier. The liberalization reform is captured with a dummy d_t, which takes a value of 0 before 1991 and a value of 1 after. The coefficient on the interaction between pre-reform distance to frontier and the reform dummy (δ) indicates whether three-digit state-industries closer to the frontier grew more quickly in the post-liberalization period relative to state-industries further from frontier.

To capture state-level institutions, Aghion, Burgess, Redding, and Zilibotti use the labor regulation measure r_{it} from Besley and Burgess 2003, which codes amendments to the central 1947 Industrial Disputes Act as pro-worker, pro-employer, or neutral and cumulates these over time to give a state-level picture of changes in the industrial relations climate. These labor regulations are specific to firms in the registered manufacturing sector that are included in the Annual Survey of Industries. Aghion, Burgess, Redding, and Zilibotti are thus linking regulatory change that affects a specific sector to outcome measures in the same sector. They look at both whether the direction of regulatory change across the 1980–1997 period affected industrial performance (the η coefficient) and also whether pre-reform institutional conditions affected post-reform performance (the θ coefficient).

The key results are shown in table 4.3. The four columns show results for different performance measures. The results suggest that state industries that were closer to the frontier (which is identified as the most productive state-industry in India) before the reforms experienced faster growth after the reform than state-industries that were farther from the frontier. A common liberalization reform is thus seen to have a heterogenous impact on the same industry located in different states. The results also show that the rate of technological progress is slower in states moving in a pro-worker direction. This is evidence that the institutional environment in which firms are embedded affected productivity growth across the 1980–1997 period. What is more striking is the evidence that liberalization magnifies the negative impact of pro-worker regulations on productivity growth. This shows how greater rent extraction by workers blunts the incentives of firms to make innovative investments in order to fight entry. State-specific regulatory policies therefore have a central bearing on whether or not

Table 4.3
Liberalization and industrial performance in Indian industries (1980–1997)

	(1)	(2)	(3)	(4)
	Log TFP	Log investment	Log profits	Log output
Pre-Reform Distance* Reform	0.157***	0.539***	0.685***	0.440***
	(0.042)	(0.168)	(0.201)	(0.059)
Labor Regulation	−0.066***	−0.052	−0.236***	−0.090***
	(0.017)	(0.042)	(0.090)	(0.034)
Pre-Reform Labor Regulation* Reform	−0.035***	−0.023***	−0.043	−0.061***
	(0.011)	(0.008)	(0.032)	(0.015)
State-industry fixed effects	YES	YES	YES	YES
Year dummies	YES	YES	YES	YES
Industry-time trends	YES	YES	YES	YES
State-reform dummies	NO	NO	NO	NO
Balanced panel	NO	NO	NO	NO
Observations	22883	21494	16204	22883
R-squared	0.69	0.87	0.75	0.94

Source: Aghion, Burgess, Redding, and Zilibotti 2003, table 1.
Notes: Robust standard errors in parentheses adjusted for clustering by state. *significant at 10%; **significant at 5%; ***significant at 1%. Regressions are weighted using time-averaged state-industry employment shares. Sample is a three-dimensional panel of three-digit industries from 16 Indian states during 1980–1997. The data consists of a panel of 22,883 observations, where we condition on a minimum of ten time-series observations for each state-industry and on at least two states being active within an industry in any time period. Log TFP is log total factor productivity. Log investment is log real gross fixed capital formation in registered manufacturing in a state-industry. Log profits is log real registered manufacturing profits in a state-industry. Log output is log real registered manufacturing output in a state-industry. Pre-reform distance is pre-reform state-industry labor productivity relative to the state with the highest level of pre-reform labor productivity within the industry. Reform is a dummy that equals 0 for 1990 and earlier and equals 1 from 1991 onward. State amendments to the Industrial Disputes Act are coded 1 = pro-worker, 0 = neutral, −1 = pro-employer, and then cumulated over the pre-reform period to generate the labor regulation measure.

the same three-digit industries located in different parts of India benefit from liberalization.

4.4 Cross-Country Effects of Liberalization

A final paper that considers the impact of liberalization on productivity is Nicoletti and Scarpetta 2003. The authors relate a large number of reforms to growth in total (multi-) factor productivity. In their paper the impact of product market reforms affects the rate of

TFP convergence across countries and industries. Those countries and industries experiencing the greatest reform experience temporarily faster growth rates while they catch up to the international steady-state growth rate. The specific question they address is whether the different patterns of reform across countries can help explain the differences in growth rates across countries and industries. They highlight two main effects of reform: Lowering entry barriers and state control are associated with faster catch-up to the frontier in manufacturing industries, with industries furthest behind the frontier getting the greatest rewards, and the process of privatization is associated with productivity gains.

The empirical approach follows Griffith, Redding, and Van Reenen (2000, 2004), who derive a model of productivity growth and catch-up from an endogenous growth framework. Nicoletti and Scarpetta replace the role of R&D in this approach with measures of product market regulation. Thus product market regulation affects an industry's TFP growth both directly and when interacted with the industry's distance to the world technological frontier. The general model is

$$\Delta \ln TFP_{it} = \alpha \Delta \ln TFP(frontier)_{it} + \beta_1 \ln TFPgap_{it}$$

$$+ (\beta_2 + \beta_3 \ln TFPgap_{it})PMR_i,$$

where PMR is an index of various indicators of product market regulation, and the coefficients are usually allowed to vary between manufacturing and service industries.

Nicoletti and Scarpetta's main results stem from the interaction between product market regulation (PMR) and the technology gap, which the authors interpret as indicating that stricter PMR delays the process of technology adoption in countries that lag behind the frontier. Here the primary impact of product market reforms and regulations is on the rate of technology transfer. Nicoletti and Scarpetta use a panel of seventeen manufacturing and six business services industries in eighteen OECD countries over the period 1984–1998.

The first set of results include a country-level, non-time-varying summary measure of regulation (combining state control and barriers to entry), as well as a country-level, time-varying measure of overall privatization. These are shown in table 4.4. The results in the second and third columns show that regulation on its own has no impact on TFP growth. In the fourth and fifth columns, the indicator for regulation is interacted with the technology gap (or distance to the frontier).

The coefficient suggests that regulation acts to slow down the process of technological catch-up.

Several issues arise with the use of these PMR indicators. First, the fact that the regulation indicators do not vary across industries or over time means that country fixed effect, which would control for unobservable country characteristics on growth, cannot be included in the regressions. Identification of the coefficients therefore comes from cross-section variation across countries in the average growth rate of TFP. No significant results are found until the regulation indicators are interacted with the technology gap measure. Given that the regulation measures are not significant on their own, it would be possible to reintroduce country dummies to check that the interaction result is robust to unobservable persistent differences across countries. However, this remains to be done.

Second, the regulation measures used in Nicoletti and Scarpetta 2003 capture the situation in 1998, which is at the end of the sample period. The underlying assumption is that end-of-period values are representative of the cross-country patterns of regulation over the entire 1984–1998 period. This will not be true if some countries have liberalized their markets faster than others. This makes causal interpretations of the results somewhat problematic.

Overall, the results that appear relatively robust are the positive effect of overall privatization and entry liberalization in services on economywide TFP growth. The latter is problematic due to the summary nature of the measure of entry liberalization, as discussed previously. The interactions of PMR measures with the technology gap suggest that the negative effects of higher PMRs on TFP growth may be greater in countries that lie furthest behind the technological frontier, in contrast to the findings by Aghion, Blundell, Griffith, Howitt, and Prantl (2003) and Aghion, Burgess, Redding, and Zilibotti (2003).

More recently, Alesina et al. (2003) have looked at the effects of entry barriers and public ownership on investment in transport, communication, and utilities sectors. The main finding from their panel regression across twelve OECD countries over the period 1975–1998, which is consistent with our own findings in Aghion, Burgess, Redding, and Zilibotti 2003, is that liberalization of entry and privatization both had an overall positive impact on long-run capital investment in these sectors. However, Alesina et al. do not distinguish between incumbent

Table 4.4
MFP regressions: The role of aggregate indicators of regulation and privatization

	Dependent variable: ΔMFP_{ijt}					
	1	2	3	4	5	6
Constant	−0.10**	−0.005	−0.01	−0.01	−0.01	−0.11***
	(0.04)	(0.01)	(0.01)	(0.01)	(0.01)	(0.04)
ΔMFP Leader$_{it}$ (MAN)	−0.01	−0.01	−0.01	−0.01	−0.01	−0.01
	(0.01)	(0.01)	(0.01)	(0.01)	(0.01)	(0.01)
ΔMFP Leader$_{it}$ (SERV)	0.08***	0.08***	0.08***	0.07***	0.08***	0.08***
	(0.02)	(0.01)	(0.01)	(0.01)	(0.01)	(0.02)
Technology gap$_{ijt-1}$ (MAN)	−0.03***	−0.02***	−0.02***	−0.04***	−0.03***	−0.03***
	(0.00)	(0.005)	(0.005)	(0.01)	(0.01)	(0.01)
Technology gap$_{ijt-1}$ (SERV)	−0.05***	−0.04***	−0.04***	−0.06***	−0.06***	−0.05***
	(0.01)	(0.01)	(0.01)	(0.01)	(0.01)	(0.01)
Human capital i$_{it}$	0.16**	0.02*	0.02	0.02	0.02	0.17**
	(0.07)	(0.01)	(0.01)	(0.01)	(0.01)	(0.07)
Regulation$_i$		−0.01		0.01		
		(0.005)		(0.01)		
Regulation$_i$* Technology gap$_{ijt-1}$				0.02**		
				(0.01)		
Regulation$_i$ (state control)			−0.01		0.01	
			(0.01)		(0.01)	
Regulation$_i$ (barriers to entrep.)			0.00		0.00	
			(0.01)		(0.01)	
Regulation$_i$ (state control)* Technology gap$_{ijt-1}$					0.02***	
					(0.01)	
Regulation$_{it}$ (time-varying)						−0.08***
						(0.021)
Regulation$_{it}$ (time-varying)* Technology gap$_{ijt-1}$						0.01
						(0.011)
Overall privatisation$_{it}$	0.25***	0.16**	0.17**	0.13*	0.14**	0.16
	(0.10)	(0.07)	(0.07)	(0.07)	(0.07)	(0.10)
Number of observations	3101	3101	3101	3101	3101	3101
Country dummies	Yes	No	No	No	No	Yes
Reset[1]	0.42	2.15*	2.41*	1.72	2.59*	0.56

Source: Nicoletti and Scarpetta 2003, table 6.
Notes: *** denotes significance at the 1% level; ** at 5% level; * at 10% level.
   Robust standard errors in equation 1 and 6; adjusted standard errors for clustering in equations 2–5.
   Samples are adjusted for outliers.
   All equations include industry and time dummies.
   Indicators of privatization measure the change in private ownership and indicators of product market regulation are increasing in the degree of restrictions imposed on market mechanisms.
[1] Ramsey's omitted-variable test: F-test on the joint significance of the additional terms in a model augmented with the second, third, and fourth powers of the predicted values of the original model.

firms and new entrants in each sector, nor do they distinguish between developed and less developed sectors.

Finally, based on a panel regression covering twenty OECD countries over the period 1980–2002, Nicoletti and Scarpetta (2004) find a positive and significant effect of entry liberalization on long-run employment rates, and all the more when labor markets are themselves less regulated (or more pro-employee). This latter finding is fully consistent with the complementarity result in Aghion, Burgess, Redding, and Zilibotti 2003.

4.5 Conclusion

Our explorer now has a better sense of the reasons why the world has tended to divide into those who are for and those who are against the liberalization of entry. While empirical findings at the aggregate level show an overall positive effect of entry on innovation and productivity growth, we also found evidence that liberalization should enhance performance to a larger extent in firms or industries that are initially closer to the technological frontier, whereas it has a negligible or even negative impact on innovation in sectors far below the technological frontier. This, in turn, suggests that complementary policies can be designed to encourage technological upgrading, either by existing firms or by reallocation of workers from low- to high-productivity firms. Similarly, the finding by Aghion, Burgess, Redding, and Zilibotti that pro-worker labor regulations may act as a brake on the potential positive impact of liberalization points to key complementarities between liberalizing product and labor markets. Domestic policy reforms can thus play a central role in determining the extent to which firms and industries benefit from macroeconomic reforms that lower barriers to entry.

A key insight from our analysis in this chapter is that there are both winners and losers from liberalization. This helps us understand why liberalization itself is often opposed, even if its overall impact is positive. Even if liberalization happens in the sense of reducing barriers to entry, groups or industries that would potentially lose from it may act as a barrier to complementary institutional reforms, thus further reducing the overall impact of liberalization on economic performance. Working out a set of liberalization reforms, which are both growth-enhancing and politically feasible, is an important subject for future research.

Epilogue

Our explorer now sits back in the cool shade of a tree to contemplate what she has learned in her travels. First, the apparent contradiction between the theory and empirics of the effects of competition on innovation and growth, has, to some extent, been resolved. The contradiction arose because early theoretical models placed too much emphasis on the impact of competition on post-innovation rents. However, integrating some key insights from the IO literature on preemption and vertical differentiation made it possible to construct growth models in which competition affects both pre- and post-innovation rents, so that it can have a positive effect on innovation and growth in addition to the Schumpeterian effect previously emphasized by the literature.

Second, contrary to what is sometimes claimed by scholars and policy advisers interested in the interplay between competition and innovation, the two notions of "competition *in* markets" (which corresponds to our measures of product market competition) and "competition *for* markets" (which captures both entry and the ability to escape current markets by creating new ones) are not contradictory. The opposite is true: They complement each other in inducing strong escape competition effects that result in higher rates of innovation.[32] This in turn has important policy implications, which brings us to our next conclusion.

Third, some commentators have argued there is a specificity of innovative markets with respect to competition. They see the role of antitrust action in innovative sectors as one of counteracting incumbent firms that try to prevent innovation by new entrants by issuing and accumulating (unjustified) patents. In other words, antitrust action should focus on fostering competition *for* the market, but not so much on increasing competition *in* the market, since this would reduce innovation incentives by reducing rents. In innovative markets where

incumbents innovate, antitrust action should be restrained so as not
to stamp out monopoly power in such markets.[33] Instead, our analysis
suggests that stimulating competition in the market, especially in sectors that are close to the corresponding world frontier and/or where
incumbent innovators are neck-and-neck, can also foster competition
for the market through the escape competition effect.[34] Incumbent
firms innovate precisely as a response to increased product market
competition or to increased entry threat, at least up to some level.
True, we also found an inverted-U relationship between competition
and growth. An interesting but difficult question is to compare the
actual level of competition in an industry to the maximum of the corresponding inverted U in order to assess whether competition at a
given point in time is too low or too high.

While not explicitly modeled, another implication of our analysis
concerns the interplay between the patent design and competition policy. As emphasized by other commentators,[35] patent breadth should be
high enough to guarantee adequate rents to innovators, but not so high
that it prevents innovation by new entrants. Again, the focus there is
entirely on competition *for* the market. Now, having made her way
through this book, our observer would suggest that patent protection
should reward new technological improvements, but without discouraging small improvements after a while so that laggard firms can always catch up with the leaders in the same industry: This in turn
would produce more neck-and-neck sectors in steady state, and therefore more intense innovation on average in the economy. But in addition, our analysis points to the importance of facilitating entry and of
fighting against collusion among incumbent firms, as complementary
stimuli for innovation.

Finally, our observer has learned that the impact of competition and
entry on innovation varies with the dispersion of technology in use
within an industry, with the industry's overall distance to the technological frontier, and she got the sense that the interaction with other
institutions such as labor markets or capital markets is also important,
although more investigation is necessary. For example, an old Schumpeterian explanation for the positive correlation between market
power and innovation is that firms are credit-constrained and that monopoly rents provide a source of internal finance. A similar argument
has been put forward to explain why new entrants do not grow as
large in Europe as in the United States.[36] However, there are alternative explanations for this latter fact: for example, differences in labor

market legislations (the fact that larger firms face more labor market restrictions in Europe) or differences in market concentration and in the political power of incumbent firms (these might be larger in Europe than in the United States). Learning more about the relative importance of these various explanations, and understanding more about the interplay between competition policy and slower-moving institutions in labor and capital markets, is one of the many challenges that still lie ahead in the process of eventually coming up with practical guidelines for policy advising in innovative sectors.

Notes

1. Between 1945 and 1968, per worker GDP was growing at an average annual rate of 3.9 percent in Mexico and 5.3 percent in Peru.

2. Some authors have argued that the if we consider GDP per hour, rather than per capita, then the European Union is at par with, if not ahead of, the United States (see Schreyer and Pilat 2001). Undoubtedly part of the difference in per capita GDP between the European Union and the United States is explained by differences in the number of hours worked. However, recent work has suggested that when differences in the skill composition of the workforce, and other factors, are accounted for, GDP of the European Union lies at around 80 percent of that of the United States (see Cette 2004).

3. In particular, Gilbert and Newbery 1982 and Fudenberg and Tirole 1986.

4. Note that π^m is greater than the initial monopoly rent the incumbent obtains from the first outlet.

5. Competition policy, of course, also has static efficiency objectives of reducing the inefficiencies of monopoly pricing.

6. If no innovation succeeds, then some firm will produce domestically but with no cost advantage over the fringe because everyone is able to produce last period's intermediate input at a constant marginal cost of unity.

7. Cohen and Levin (1989) provide a comprehensive survey of the literature. See also the review by Kamien and Schwartz (1972).

8. There is some evidence that very small firms, for example, those not listed on the stock market, also do a substantial amount of R&D. See, inter alia, Pavitt, Robson, and Townsend 1987.

9. See, inter alia, Scherer 1965a,b.

10. Cohen and Levin 1989 provide a good discussion of these issues.

11. This point is emphasized by Demsetz (1973).

12. There is a substantial literature on the econometric issues involved. See Nickell 1981 for a discussion of the bias in within-groups estimator. See Arellano and Bond 1991 for a discussion of first differences. See Arellano and Bover 1995 and Blundell and Bond 1998 for a discussion of the GMM Systems estimator.

13. He argues that all theoretical parameterizations of competition share two features known as the reallocation effect: A rise in competition raises the profits of a firm relative

to the profits of a less efficient firm; a rise in competition reduces the profits of the least efficient firm active in the industry. He therefore proposes an alternative measure based on the ratio of profits between more and less efficient firms.

14. For example, the difficulties in using concentration indexes is illustrated with data from the U.K. pharmaceutical industry. In the United Kingdom the pharmaceutical industry is dominated by two large players, GlaxoSmithKline and AstraZeneca, whose sales accounts for about 65 percent and 30 percent of the market. But these firms are global players, competing with other U.S. and European firms. In global terms they have market shares of 7 percent and 4 percent; these low market shares in turn reflect the fierce competition in the industry. In this case, without global market sales, concentration measures would be extremely misleading.

15. See Griliches 1990 for a comprehensive treatment of this issue.

16. This method assumes that valuable patents are cited more frequently by other patents than lower-value patents. Each patent is weighted by the number of citations it receives, thus helping to measure the importance or quality of the patent. See, for example, Jaffe 1986.

17. See Robson, Townsend, and Pavitt 1988 for details.

18. See, inter alia, Hall 1988, Klette and Griliches 1996, and Klette 1999.

19. These two articles are chosen because they raise interesting issues for discussion here. Geroski 1995 also considered these issues, although using industry-level data. Geroski found a negative correlation: More competition (lower concentration) is associated with more innovation. What is important about his papers is that they were among the first to control for a range of industry-level characteristics that may be correlated with market structure.

20. Nickell used firm-level panel data including 978 observations on 147 stock market–listed firms from 1975 to 1986.

21. Nickell uses different coefficient estimates than those reported in the text to calculate this index. He uses $\phi_5 = -0.16$ and $\phi_6 = -0.053$. These are estimated using a large sample of firms.

22. Data includes 3,511 observations on 340 stock market–listed firms over the period 1972–1982.

23. See Megginsom and Netter 2001 for a recent survey.

24. The idea of allowing for incumbent innovation, and of looking at the difference between pre- and post-innovation rents, is directly inspired from the preemption literature mentioned in chapter 1.

25. See Cohen and Levin 1989 (p. 1075) for a brief discussion of this earlier literature.

26. This section borrows unrestrainedly from Aghion and Howitt 2004, which itself builds on Aghion, Harris, and Vickers 1997, Aghion, Harris, Howitt, and Vickers 2001, and the discrete-time version of the Schumpeterian growth model (see Acemoglu, Aghion, and Zilibotti 2003) used in the previous chapters.

27. This, in turn, follows immediately from the fact that

$$\frac{\partial y_t}{\partial x_{it}} = \chi = p_{it},$$

which in turn implies that in equilibrium

$$x_{it} = \left(\frac{\chi}{\alpha}\right)^{1/(\alpha-1)} A_{it}.$$

We then simply substitute for x_{it} in the expression for profit π_t, namely,

$$\pi_t = (p_{it} - 1)x_{it} = (\chi - 1)\left(\frac{\chi}{\alpha}\right)^{1/(\alpha-1)} A_{it}.$$

28. A recent paper by Vives (2004) points to an effect that is quite similar to our escape competition effect. In that paper, higher product market competition in the form of higher demand elasticity encourages firms to invest more in cost reduction in order to steal more demand from other firms by charging lower prices. So what competition does is to reduce the residual demand for firms that do not innovate, while increasing the demand for firms that achieved lower costs.

29. The data are on U.K.-listed firms over the period 1968–1997 and include information on costs, sales, investments, and the number of successful patent applications at the U.S. Patent Office. Detailed information on citations are used to weight the measure of patents granted for each firm in each year.

30. See Ai and Chen 2003.

31. The main sample used by Aghion, Blundell, Griffith, Howitt, and Prantl for estimating productivity growth models is a panel of 17,741 observations on 2,944 domestic incumbent establishments in the ARD between 1987 and 1993. The main firm panel for estimating innovation models consists of 1,101 observations on 179 firms in the IFS-Leverhume database. All firms in this sample are considered to be incumbent firms since firms listed on the London Stock Exchange are all large and old. About 60 percent of the firms in this sample are patenting firms between 1987 and 1993.

32. This distinction between "competition in markets" and "competition for markets" is emphasized by Geroski (2001), but it also underlies the recent Federal Trade Commission Report entitled "To Promote Competition: The Proper Balance of Competition and Patent Law and Policy" (http://www.ftc.gov/os/2003/10/innovationrpt.pdf).

33. See, for example, Etro 2004.

34. This view is shared by some policymakers; see, for example, Vickers 2001.

35. See, for example, Shapiro 2002.

36. See, for example, Nicoletti and Scarpetta 2003.

References

Acemoglu, D., P. Aghion, and F. Zilibotti. 2003. "Distance to Frontier, Selection and Economic Growth." NBER Working Paper 9066.

Aggerwal, R., and A. Sandwick. 1999. "Executive Compensation, Strategic Competition, and Relative Performance Evaluation: Theory and Evidence." *The Journal of Finance* 54: 1999–2043.

Aghion, P., N. Bloom, R. Blundell, R. Griffith, and P. Howitt. 2003. "Competition and Innovation: An Inverted U Relationship." NBER Working Paper No. 9269.

Aghion, P., R. Blundell, R. Griffith, P. Howitt, and S. Prantl. 2003. "Entry and Productivity Growth: Evidence from Micro-Level Panel Data." *Journal of the European Economic Association, Papers and Proceedings* 2: 265–276.

Aghion, P., R. Blundell, R. Griffith, P. Howitt, and S. Prantl. 2004. "Entry and Distance to the Frontier." IFS Working Paper.

Aghion, P., R. Burgess, S. Redding, and F. Zilibotti. 2003. "The Unequal Effects of Liberalization: Theory and Evidence from India." Mimeo.

Aghion, P., M. Dewatripont, and P. Rey. 1999. "Corporate Governance, Competition Policy and Industrial Policy." *European Economic Review* 41: 797–805.

Aghion, P., C. Harris, P. Howitt, and J. Vickers. 2001. "Competition, Imitation and Growth with Step-by-Step Innovation." *Review of Economic Studies* 68: 467–492.

Aghion, P., C. Harris, and J. Vickers. 1997. "Competition and Growth with Step-by-Step Innovation: An Example." *European Economic Review* 41: 771–782.

Aghion, P., and P. Howitt. 1992. "A Model of Growth through Creative Destruction." *Econometrica* 60: 323–351.

Aghion, P., and P. Howitt. 1998. *Endogenous Growth Theory*. Cambridge, MA: MIT Press.

Aghion, P., and P. Howitt. 2004. "Growth with Quality-Improving Innovations: An Integrated Framework." Forthcoming in *The Handbook of Economic Growth*, ed. P. Aghion and S. Durlauf. Amsterdam: Elsevier.

Aghion, P., and M. Schankerman. 2003. "On the Welfare Effects and Political Economy of Competition-Enhancing Policies."

Ai, C., and X. Chen. 2003. "Efficient Estimation of Models with Conditional Moment Restrictions Containing Unknown Functions." *Econometrica* 71, no. 6: 1795–1843.

Alesina, A., S. Ardagna, G. Nicoletti, and F. Schiantarelli. 2003. "Regulation and Investment." NBER Working Paper No. 9560.

Arellano, M., and S. Bond. 1991. "Some Test of Specification for Panel Data: Monte Carlo Evidence and an Application to Employment Equations." *Review of Economic Studies* 58: 277–297.

Arellano, M., and O. Bover. 1995. "Another Look at the Instrumental-Variable Estimation of Error-Components Models." *Journal of Econometrics* 68: 29–51.

Arrow, Kenneth. 1962. "The Economic Implications of Learning-by-Doing." *Review of Economic Studies* 29, no. 1: 155–173.

Besley, T., and R. Burgess. 2003. "Halving Global Poverty." *Journal of Economic Perspectives* 17, no. 3 (Summer): 3–22.

Blundell, R., and S. Bond. 1998. "Initial Conditions and Moment Conditions in Dynamic Panel Data Models." *Journal of Econometrics* 87, no. 1 (Nov.): 115–143.

Blundell, R., R. Griffith, and J. Van Reenen. 1995. "Dynamic Count Data Models of Technological Innovation." *Economic Journal* 105 (March): 333–344.

Blundell, R., R. Griffith, and J. Van Reenen. 1999. "Market Share, Market Value and Innovation in a Panel of British Manufacturing Firms." *Review of Economic Studies* 66: 529–554.

Boone, J. 2000. "Measuring Product Market Competition." CEPR Working Paper 2636.

Caves, R. 1974. "Multinational Firms, Competition and Productivity in Host-Country Markets." *Economica* 41, no. 162 (May): 176–193.

Cette, G. 2004. "Is Hourly Labour Productivity Structurally Higher in Some Major European Countries Than It Is in the United States?" Available at www.csls.ca/events/cea2004/cette.pdf.

Cohen, W., and R. Levin. 1989. "Empirical Studies of Innovation and Market Structure." In *Handbook of Industrial Organization, Volume II*, ed. R. Schmalensee and R. Willig, 1059–1107. Amsterdam: Elsevier Science.

Dasgupta, P., and J. Stiglitz. 1980. "Industrial Structure and the Nature of Innovative Activity." *The Economic Journal* 90, no. 358 (June): 266–293.

Demsetz, H. 1973. "Industry Structure, Market Rivalry, and Public Policy." *Journal of Law and Economy* 16 (April): 1–9.

Dixit, A., and J. Stiglitz. 1977. "Monopolistic Competition and Optimum Product Diversity." *The American Economic Review* 67, no. 3 (June): 297–308.

Encaoua, D., and A. Hollander. 2002. "Competition Policy and Innovation." *Oxford Review of Economic Policy* 18: 63–79.

Encaoua, D., and D. Ulph. 2000. "Catching-Up or Leapfrogging? The Effects of Competition on Innovation and Growth." Universite Paris I, EUREQua Working Paper 2000.97.

Etro, F. 2004. "Innovation by Leaders." *Economic Journal* 114: 281–303.

Fudenberg, D., and J. Tirole. 1986. "A 'Signal-Jamming' Theory of Predation." *RAND Journal of Economics* 17, no. 3 (Autumn): 366–376.

Geroski, P. 1995. *Market Structure, Corporate Performance and Innovative Activity*. Oxford: Oxford University Press.

Geroski, P. 2001. "Competition for Markets." Paper presented at Workshop on Market Definition, London, May 10.

Geroski, P., S. Machin, and J. Van Reenen. 1993. "The Profitability of Innovating Firms." *RAND Journal of Economics* 24, no. 2: 198–211.

Gerschenkron, A. 1962. *Economic Backwardness in Historical Perspective*. Cambridge, MA: Harvard University Press.

Gilbert, R., and D. Newbery. 1982. "Preemptive Patenting and the Persistence of Monopoly." *American Economic Review* 72: 514–526.

Griffith, R., S. Redding, and J. Van Reenen. 2000. "R&D and Absorptive Capacity: From Theory to Data." *The Scandinavian Journal of Economics* 105, no. 1: 99–118.

Griffith, R., S. Redding, and J. Van Reenen. 2004. "Mapping the Two Faces of R&D: Productivity Growth in a Panel of OECD Industries." *Review of Economics and Statistics* 86, no. 4: 883–895.

Griliches, Z. 1990. "Patent Statistics as Economic Indicators: A Survey." *Journal of Economic Literature* 28: 1661–1707.

Grossfeld, I., and T. Tressel. 2001. "Competition and Corporate Governance: Substitutes or Complements? Evidence from the Warsaw Stock Exchange." Working Paper DELTA.

Grossman, G., and E. Helpman. 1991. *Innovation and Growth in the Global Economy*. Cambridge, MA: MIT Press.

Hall, R. 1988. "The Relationship between Price and Marginal Cost in U.S. Industry." *Journal of Political Economy* 96: 921–947.

Hart, O. 1983. "The Market Mechanism as an Incentive Scheme." *Bell Journal of Economics* 14 (Autumn): 366–382.

Holmstrom, B. 1999. "Managerial Incentive Problems: A Dynamic Perspective." *Review of Economic Studies* 66: 169–182.

Jaffe, A. 1986. "Technological Opportunity and Spillovers of R&D: Evidence from Firms' Patents, Profits and Market Value." *American Economic Review* 76: 984–1001.

Jagannathan, R., and S. B. Srinivasan. 1999. "Does Product Market Competition Reduce Agency Costs?" *North American Journal of Economics and Finance* 10: 387–399.

Kamien, M., and N. Schwartz. 1972. "Timing of Innovations under Rivalry." *Econometrica* 40: 43–60.

Klette, T., and Z. Griliches. 1996. "The Inconsistency of Common Scale Estimators When Output Prices Are Unobserved and Endogenous." *Journal of Applied Econometrics* 11, no. 4: 343–361.

Klette, T. J. 1999. "Market Power, Scale Economies and Productivity: Estimates from a Panel of Establishment Data." *Journal of Industrial Economics* 47, no. 4: 451–476.

Leech, D., and J. Leahy. 1991. "Ownership Structure, Control Type Classifications and the Performance of Large British Companies." *Economic Journal* 101: 1418–1437.

Levin, R., W. Cohen, and D. Mowery. 1985. "R&D Appropriability, Opportunity, and Market Structure: New Evidence on Some Schumpeterian Hypotheses." *American Economic Review Proceedings* 75: 20–24.

Mayes, D., and P. Hart. 1994. *The Single Market Programme as a Stimulus to Change: Comparisons between Britain and Germany*. Cambridge: Cambridge University Press.

Megginsom, W., and J. Netter. 2001. "From State to Market: A Survey of Empirical Studies on Privatization." *Journal of Economic Literature* 39: 321–389.

Nickell, S. 1981. "Biases in Dynamic Models with Fixed Effects." *Econometrica* 49: 1417–1426.

Nickell, S. 1996. "Competition and Corporate Performance." *Journal of Political Economy* 104, no. 4: 724–746.

Nickell, S., and D. Nicolitsas. 1999. "How Does Financial Pressure Affect Firms?" *European Economic Review* 43: 1435–1456.

Nickell, S., D. Nicolitsas, and N. Dryden. 1997. "What Makes Firms Perform Well?" *European Economic Review* 43: 783–796.

Nickell, S., D. Nicolitsas, and M. Patterson. 2001. "Does Doing Badly Encourage Management Innovation?" *Oxford Bulletin of Economics and Statistics* 63: 5–28.

Nicoletti, G., and S. Scarpetta. 2003. "Regulation, Productivity and Growth." *Economic Policy* 36: 11–72.

Nicoletti, G., and S. Scarpetta. 2004. "Regulation and Employment, Evidence from OECD Countries." OECD Working Paper.

Pavitt, K., M. Robson, and J. Townsend. 1987. "The Size Distribution of Innovating Firms in the UK: 1945–83." *Journal of Industrial Economics* 35: 297–316.

Pesaran, M. H., and R. Smith. 1995. "Estimating Long-Run Relationships from Dynamic Heterogeneous Panels." *Journal of Econometrics* 68: 79–113.

Robson, M., J. Townsend, and K. Pavitt. 1988. "Sectoral Patterns of Production and Use of Innovations in the UK: 1945–83." *Research Policy* 17: 1–14.

Romer, P. 1990. "Endogenous Technological Change." *Journal of Political Economy* 98, no. 2: S71–S102.

Salop, S. 1977. "The Noisy Monopolist: Imperfect Information, Price Dispersion, and Price Discrimination." *Review of Economic Studies* 44: 393–406.

Sapir, André. 2004. *An Agenda for a Growing Europe: The Sapir Report*. New York: Oxford University Press.

Scharfstein, D. 1988. "Product-Market Competition and Managerial Slack." *RAND Journal of Economics* 19, no. 1 (Spring): 147–155.

Scherer, F. 1965a. "Corporate Inventive Output, Profits and Growth." *Journal of Political Economy* 73, no. 3: 290–297.

Scherer, F. 1965b. "Firm Size, Market Structure, Opportunity and the Output of Patented Inventions." *American Economic Review* 55, no. 5: 1097–1125.

Schmidt, K. 1997. "Managerial Incentives and Product Market Competition." *Review of Economic Studies* 64: 191–213.

Schreyer, P., and D. Pilat. 2001. "Measuring Productivity." OECD Economic Studies No. 33, 2001/2, OECD, Paris.

Schumpeter, J. 1943. *Capitalism, Socialism and Democracy*. London: Allen Unwin.

Shapiro, C. 2002. "Competition Policy and Innovation." DSTI/DOC(2002)11, OECD.

Tirole, J. 1988. *The Theory of Industrial Organization*. Cambridge, MA: MIT Press.

van Ark, B., R. Inklaar, and R. H. McGuckin. 2002. "Changing Gear: Productivity, ICT and Service: Europe and the United States." EPKE-WP-02. Available at www.niesr.ac .uk/epke/bart2.pdf.

Vickers, J. 2001. "Competition Policy and Innovation." Paper presented at International Competition Policy Conference, Oxford, June 27, 2001. Available at http://www.oft.gov .uk/NR/rdonlyres/4DE9CB9E-88BE-4A04-8E1B-4AF7DED72B46/0/spe0701.pdf.

Vives, X. 2004. "Innovation and Competitive Pressure." Mimeo, INSEAD.

Index